★ 职业教育城市轨道交通专业精品教材 ★

Chengshi Guidao Jiaotong Zhuanye Yingyu
城市轨道交通专业英语
（第2版）

石启菊　沈鹏远　主　编
刘春红　庄　静　副主编
　　　　陆洪波　主　审

人民交通出版社股份有限公司
北　京

内 容 提 要

本书为职业教育城市轨道交通专业精品教材。书中从企业岗位需求和教学实践出发，精心设置基础篇、运营篇、设施篇和车辆篇4个模块，共20个教学单元，每一个单元内容精炼，采用了大量的图片，图文并茂，尽力为学生提供生动形象的学习资料。

本书为职业教育城市轨道交通专业及相关专业的教材和教学参考用书，也可供相关人员使用，还可以作为相关岗前培训教材。

图书在版编目（CIP）数据

城市轨道交通专业英语/石启菊，沈鹏远主编. —2版. —北京：人民交通出版社股份有限公司，2021.7
ISBN 978-7-114-17322-6

Ⅰ.①城… Ⅱ.①石…②沈… Ⅲ.①城市铁路—轨道交通—英语—中等专业学校—教材 Ⅳ.①U239.5

中国版本图书馆 CIP 数据核字（2021）第 088364 号

书　　名：	**城市轨道交通专业英语**（第2版）
著 作 者：	石启菊　沈鹏远
责任编辑：	时　旭　侯力文
责任校对：	孙国靖　卢　弦
责任印制：	张　凯
出版发行：	人民交通出版社股份有限公司
地　　址：	（100011）北京市朝阳区安定门外外馆斜街3号
网　　址：	http://www.ccpcl.com.cn
销售电话：	（010）59757973
总 经 销：	人民交通出版社股份有限公司发行部
经　　销：	各地新华书店
印　　刷：	北京市密东印刷有限公司
开　　本：	787×1092　1/16
印　　张：	10.75
字　　数：	181千
版　　次：	2011年6月　第1版
	2021年7月　第2版
印　　次：	2023年7月　第2版　第2次印刷　总第15次印刷
书　　号：	ISBN 978-7-114-17322-6
定　　价：	43.00元

（有印刷、装订质量问题的图书，由本公司负责调换）

Preface 第2版前言

随着我国城镇化规模不断扩大,流动人口与机动车数量快速增加,现有城市交通基础设施面临着巨大的挑战。城市轨道交通对改善现代城市交通拥堵局面,调整和优化城市区域布局,促进国民经济发展发挥的作用已是不容置疑的客观现实。在城市化进程加快、新一线城市经济崛起的背景下,我国城市轨道交通迎来快速发展,城市轨道交通运营规模不断扩大,城市轨道交通运营人才需求问题也亟待解决。

本套城市轨道专业教材自2010年出版以来,在教学、科研和培训工作中发挥了很大的作用,深受使用院校师生的好评。为体现城市轨道交通发展中新技术、新材料、新设备、新工艺和新标准的应用,更好地适应职业教育"校企合作,工学结合"的人才培养模式,满足实际教学需求,人民交通出版社股份有限公司根据使用院校师生反馈的意见和建议,组织相关专业教师、企业技术人员,对本套教材进行了全面修订。

随着国际化都市的建设和发展,对轨道从业人员的英语应用能力要求也越来越高。但是目前针对城市轨道交通专业的英语教材依然贫乏,本教材就是在此背景下编写而成。

本教材以岗位需求为前提,寻求不同的知识载体,设置各种各样的工作任务,以学生为主体,教师为主导的方式,引领学生学习。结合学生的认知规律,构建不同的任务情境,发挥学生的主观能动性,在学中做、在做中学,感受收获知识的乐趣。在教学组织的过程中,让学生在循序渐进完成工作任务的过程中既掌握知识,又掌握学习和工作的方法和态度,并提高与人沟通、合作的能力。在编写的过程中,尽量结合岗位中常见的、重点的词汇和功能句型进行了灵活的连接,把零散的重点知识系统化,便于学生积累和翻阅查找。本书末尾还附有城市轨道交通专业常用的词汇术语,以便学生参考和记忆。

本次修订工作由常州交通职业学院老师编写完成:刘春红负责 PART ONE 内容

和附录的编写,庄静负责 PART TWO 内容编写,石启菊和沈鹏远负责 PART THREE 和 PART FOUR 内容编写,张秋芬和姚洁负责附录和插图的整理、排版。全书由石启菊和沈鹏远负责统稿,由陆洪波主审。

限于编者水平,书中难免有疏漏和错误之处,恳请广大读者提出宝贵建议,以便进一步修改和完善。

编 者
2021 年 2 月

Contents 目录

PART ONE   BASIC PART 基础篇 1
- Unit 1   Greeting Passengers and Making Introductions 问候与介绍 2
- Unit 2   Thanks and Apologies 感谢与致歉 10
- Unit 3   Providing Information and Offering Help 提供信息和帮助 17
- Unit 4   Asking the Way and Giving Directions 问路和指路 24
- Unit 5   Step into the Subway 步入地铁 32

PART TWO   OPERATIONAL PART 运营篇 41
- Unit 6   Station Equipment 车站设备 42
- Unit 7   Station Service 车站服务 50
- Unit 8   Tickets 票务 57
- Unit 9   Broadcasting 地铁广播 65
- Unit 10 Security 安全运营 74

PART THREE   FACILITIES PART 设施篇 83
- Unit 11 Definition of the Metro System 地铁系统定义 84
- Unit 12 Third Rail of a Metro System 地铁系统轨道 90
- Unit 13 Metro Stations 地铁站 97
- Unit 14 Platforms 站台 104
- Unit 15 Metro Depot Facilities 地铁回车场设施 111

PART FOUR   VEHICLE PART 车辆篇 119
- Unit 16 Electric Locomotive 电力机车 120
- Unit 17 Bogies 转向架 128
- Unit 18 Pantographs 受电弓 135
- Unit 19 Pneumatic Brakes 气压制动 141
- Unit 20 Maintenance and Management 维护与管理 148

Appendix　附录 ·· 153
　附录1：地下铁道列车车票使用办法 ·· 153
　附录2：英文数字、算式表示法 ·· 155
　附录3：公共信息中英文对照 ·· 156
　附录4：常用缩略语 ·· 158

参考文献 ·· 163

PART ONE BASIC PART
基 础 篇

Unit 1 Greeting Passengers and Making Introductions 问候与介绍

Learning Objectives

After learning this unit, you should

* Understand what you will do when you meet someone;
* Master how to make introductions;
* Be able to introduce and identify yourself to others.

Advised Hours

2 class hours.

PART ONE BASIC PART 基础篇

Part A Lead-in

Tick out what will you do when you meet someone for the first time?

Shake hands	☐	Make a bow	☐
Hug etiquette	☐	Kiss of peace	☐
Say hello	☐	Smile	☐
Nod ritual	☐	Ask how old are you	☐
Fix your eyes on	☐		

How to greet people and make introductions?

1. Finding out someone's name.

   Excuse me, is your name/ are you Mr. James?

2. Introducing yourself.

Hello, I'm / my name is Tonny.

3. Introducing other people

This is / I'd like to introduce Mr. James.

Do you know/Have you met Mr. James?

4. Giving out information about other people

He is from Nanjing.

He works in the Nanjing Subway.

5. Greeting and responding

How are you? Fine, thank you. / Not too bad, thanks.

Nice to see you. / Nice to see you, too.

How do you do, Mr. Zhang? Pleased to meet you. /How do you do? Pleased to meet you, too.

(*John Ford is the company president; Wang Dan is the secretary of the foreign affairs office from China Bright Food Company. She is responsible for meeting John Ford at the railway station.*)

Wang Dan: Good morning. Are you John Ford?

John Ford: Yes, and...?

Wang Dan: Welcome to Nanjing, president Ford. I'm Wang Dan, the secretary of the foreign affairs office from China Bright Food Company. Please call me Wang Dan.

John Ford: Oh, nice to meet you, Wang Dan.

Wang Dan: Nice to meet you, too. How was the trip?

John Ford: It was ok, though I feel a bit crowded.

Wang Dan: Would you like me to help you with the luggage?

John Ford: Oh, thank you.

Wang Dan: Please follow me to the gate. The company car is waiting for you outside.

PART ONE   BASIC PART 基础篇

 New Words and Expressions

Are you...?			你是……吗？
secretary	[ˈsɛkrəˌtɛrɪ]	n.	秘书
crowded	[ˈkraʊdɪd]	adj.	拥挤的
Nice to meet you			见到你很高兴
luggage	[ˈlʌgɪdʒ]	n.	行李
outside	[ˈaʊtˈsaɪd]	adv.	在外面

 Part C Passage

Self-introduction

　　Good morning, my name is Su Pei. You can just call me Lily if you like. It is really a great honor to have this opportunity to introduce myself. I hope that I can make a good performance today. I am twenty-three years old and I live in Yancheng. I am studying Management of Rail Transit in Beijing Jiaotong University. My grades come out top in my department. I have a lot of interests, such as dancing, reading and cooking. I am familiar with computer operation and office software, which can help me do the office work very well. I am young, bright, energetic and confident. I think I'm a good team player and also I am able to work under great pressure.

That's all. It is my great pleasure to have a chance to present myself to you. Thank you!

 New Words and Expressions

honor	[ˈɒnə]	n.	荣誉
opportunity	[ˌɒpəˈtjuːnətɪ]	n.	机会
performance	[pəˈfɔːməns]	n.	表演
department	[dɪˈpɑːrtmənt]	n.	部门
Management of Rail Transit			轨道交通管理
operation	[ˌɒpəˈreɪʃn]	n.	操作
software	[ˈsɒftweə(r)]	n.	软件
energetic	[ˌenəˈdʒetɪk]	adj.	充满活力的
confident	[ˈkɒnfɪdənt]	adj.	自信的
pressure	[ˈpreʃər]	n.	压力

1. How much information is mentioned in Su Pei's self-introduction?

2. Tick out which aspect will you mention during a self-introduction?

Content	Su Pei	You	Your partner
name, age, hometown			
family			
education background			
major			
hobby or specialty			
weakness			
salary			

Try to summarize the words or expressions we used in greetings and introductions in the following form.

self-introduction, pleased to meet you, how are things, hello, let me introduce..., nice to meet you, honor, opportunity, performance, reside, personality, energetic, bright, confident, pressure, how do you do, I'd like to introduce you to..., you can call me..., pronounce your last name, train attendant, conductress, dinning car attendant, station master, dispatcher, puncher, repairman
Words or expressions for greeting people	

Words or expressions for introduction	Continue

Part E Language Use

1. Nice to meet you.

2. Are you Mr. Robinson?

3. Let me introduce myself.

4. Nice to meet you too.

5. I am a conductress of this train.

6. I'd like to know your nationality.

7. If you have any questions or difficulties while travelling, please let us know.

8. Mr. Wang, this is Mike Watson. He is from Hong Kong.

Complete the dialogues with the sentences in "try to read":

J: Jack; R: Mr. Robinson

Dialogue 1:

J: Good morning, I am Jack. _____, the HR manager of Beijing Subway Company. I am a repairman.

R: Yes, that is me. _____, Jack. Welcome on board.

J: _____. Thank you.

Dialogue 2:

C: Conductor; **P**: Passenger

C: Good morning, sir!

P: Good morning!

C: Let me introduce myself. _____. My name is Zhang Li.

P: _____. My name is George White.

C: _____. Mr. White. _____.

P: I'm American.

C: Thank you. _____.

P: Ok, thank you.

Unit 2 Thanks and Apologies
感谢与致歉

Learning Objectives

After learning this unit, you should

* Understand the importance of polite;
* Master how to express thanks and apologies to others;
* Be able to use polite language.

Advised Hours

2 class hours.

PART ONE BASIC PART 基础篇

Part A Lead-in

Tick out whom would you most like to thank?

Perhaps you don't know that today is Thanksgiving Day, a western festival for people to express their appreciations or to give gifts to their relatives, friends and any people who are important towards them. Of course, the first person I want to write a so-called thank-you letter to is my dear...

Grandfather	☐	Grandmother	☐
Father	☐	Mother	☐
Brother	☐	Sister	☐
Teacher	☐	Close friend	☐

How to express thanks and apologies?

1. Thank you so much!
   That was really nice of you!

I just wanted to thank you for...

I just want to tell you how much I appreciate (your)...

Oh, this is great! Thanks!

2. I'm sorry (to)...

   I do apologize for (what I've done).

   I must apologize.

   Please forgive me for...

   Sorry, it's my fault.

   I really don't mean...

(*Mike, Tom and Rose are going for a picnic at Qingfeng Park together. Rose is now waiting for Mike outside the Culture Palace Park Station. They are we-chatting.*)

Tom: Hello, everyone. I've got Qingfeng Park now. Where are you?

Rose: Oh, really? Good boy, you're the first.

Tom: Hello, Mike. Where are you?

Rose: I'm waiting for Mike at the Culture Palace Station.

Tom: Ok, what had happened, Mike? We're all expecting you.

Mike: Wait, wait, wait... I'm so sorry. I've been held up by the traffic jam for 20 minutes near Hongmei Park. There's a flower show here, and there are huge crowds of people. I'm trying to walk to Hongmei Park Station.

Rose: All right. Don't worry, I need to buy some pizzas and puddings.

Mike: I'm terribly sorry to keep you waiting. Plus three ice-creams, it's on me.

Rose: It doesn't matter, don't mention it.

Tom: Great. See you all.

New Words and Expressions

Culture Palace			文化宫	traffic	[ˈtræfɪk]	n.	交通
traffic jam			交通阻塞	expect	[ɪkˈspɛkt]	vt. &vi.	期待
pizza	[ˈpɪtsə]	n.	披萨	pudding	[ˈpʊdɪŋ]	n.	布丁

A letter

Shanghai Subway Station:

I come from Jiangsu Province, on July 6, 2020. When taking your Subway Line 2 to the Bund, I accidentally lost the camera on the subway after taking my temperature. I connected to Shanghai Subway Company and learned that a metro staff found my camera and had sent it to the Station Master's Office. Thanks to Shanghai Subway Station, in the first time to help me find the camera.

New Words and Expressions

province	[ˈprɔvɪns]	n.	省

temperature	[ˈtemprətʃər]	n.	体温
the Station Master's Office			站长室
accidentally	[ˌæksəˈdɛntəlɪ]	adv.	偶然地
connect	[kəˈnekt]	v.	联系

Try to understand

1. When was the camera lost in the passage?

2. Fill in the blanks:

Question	Answer
Where did I come from?	
Which line did I take?	
Who found my camera?	
Where was my camera after the staff found it?	

Part D Word Power

Try to collect

Try to guess the meaning of the following phrases and classify them into different categories. Fill in the following form.

1. I'm really sorry.   2. Forget it.   3. It was my pleasure.   4. I apologize for...   5. Thanks to you (we made it on time.)   6. I couldn't have done it without you.   7. You're (always) welcome.   8. No big deal.   9. Cut it out.   10. Please accept my heartfelt apology.   11. I beg your forgiveness.   12. I feel really bad/sorry about...   13. I am really sorry for not keeping my promise.   14. Just so so.   15. That's all right.   16. Your help was greatly appreciated.   17. Thank you for taking your time out of your (business) date.   18. Thanks for sharing.   19. Thanks in advance.   20. Thank you very much in advance.   21. I am not sure how to put it, but I'm sorry that I have done something wrong to you.   22. It must have been very embarrassing to...   23. I'll never forgive myself.   24. Will you ever forgive me?   25. How could I be so thoughtless?   26. It's all my fault.   27. I didn't mean it.   28. Thank you for everything.   29. Thank you all for coming.   30. I appreciate your help.   31. I really appreciate it.   32. I'm truly grateful for your help.   33. Thanks very much/ Thank you very much.   34. I'd like to express my gratitude.

Thanks	Apologies	Answers to them

Part E Language Use

Try to read

1. How careless of me to upset your glass of water. I'm terribly sorry.

2. Oh, thank you for your concern.

3. Hi, can I do anything to help you?

4. Thanks again. It's so kind of you.

5. Thank you for all you've done for me.

6. ... smoking is not allowed in the cabin.

7. Oh, it's a little heavy.

8. But is there a smoking compartment, please?

9. I'm sorry for causing you so much trouble.

Complete the dialogues with the sentences in "try to read":

P: passenger; S: station staff

Dialogue 1:

P: _____.

S: Sure, of course, if not too much trouble.

P: _____. Where will you go today?

S: I'm going to Changzhou.

P: Ok, it's Line 2, this way please.

S: Ok. You can lay it down here. _____. Do you need some drink?

P: No, thank you.

S: _____.

P: Oh, my pleasure. Bye.

S: See you.

Dialogue 2:

P: Excuse me, but smoking is not allowed in the cabin. Look, the woman and the little boy are coughing there.

S: Sorry. _____?

P: No, there isn't. If you want to smoke, please go between the cars. You will see an ashtray on the wall.

S: I see. _____.

PART ONE　BASIC PART 基础篇

Unit 3　Providing Information and Offering Help　提供信息和帮助

Learning Objectives

After learning this unit, you should

* Understand the importance of service;
* Master how to provide information to a visitor about subway;
* Be able to use the equipment in the subway.

Advised Hours

2 class hours.

Part A Lead-in

Try to think

How can you go to College Town from Jinghai Park?

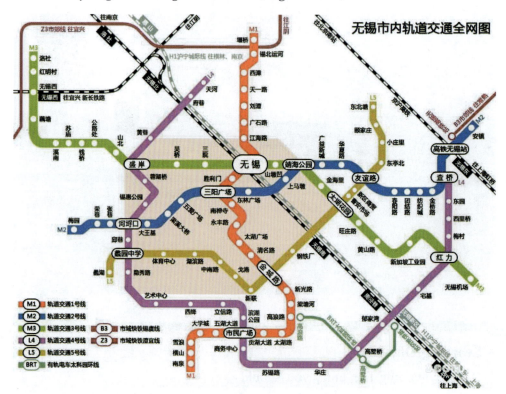

Try to discuss

Tick out which manner would you like to use to ask for the information according to "try to think"?

Navigation self-drive ☐

Ask for the information center at the subway station ☐

Ask for a stranger ☐

Ask staff member at the subway station ☐

Search the information over the Internet ☐

Part B Dialogue

(*This is the first day after Jack's arrival in Shanghai. He has lost his way. He is now at the Information Center and asks for help.*)

Jack	: Excuse me, sir. I'm a stranger here and have lost my way.
Staff member	: I'm sorry to hear that. But where do you want to go?
Jack	: I want to return to my hotel, Shanghai Jianguo Hotel.
Staff member	: Oh, just walk down this road and turn left at the first street. Then, walk four blocks and you'll find your hotel.
Jack	: Thank you, sir.
Staff member	: No problem. Actually, you can take the Subway Line 4 and get off at Shanghai Indoor Stadium Station.
Jack	: I see, but I'd rather walk.
Staff member	: All right.
Jack	: Thank you very much. Goodbye.
Staff member	: You are welcome. Bye.

 New Words and Expressions

Information Center	信息中心	block	[blɔk]	n.	街区
Shanghai Jianguo Hotel	上海建国宾馆	Shanghai Indoor Stadium Station			上海体育馆站

Part C Passage

Tips for taking subway

Subway is a very important means of transport around our city. Being fast and affordable, it is pretty much convenient not just for locals who work in the city, but also for new guys in town who want to check out different places.

Here are some tips for you if you want to use the subway. Enjoy:

1. Ask for help

The first tip might only apply to people who do not have subways in their countries and it is only their first time.

2. Use the maps

Located near exits of subway stations, maps are very important for a subway passenger in order to avoid the trouble of losing your way.

3. Always remember the right exit

You need to know the right exit that leads you to the nearest point of the place you are going to.

4. Always read the signs

Of course signs should not be taken for granted.

5. Buying a subway card is a better option

For convenience, the better option would be to buy a card, load enough money on it, so that you will not always have to lose time buying a ticket every time you want to travel.

6. Good behavior and respectful etiquettes

This is very needful.

 New Words and Expressions

| transport | [træns'pɔːt] | n. | 运输 |
| convenient | [kən'vinjənt] | adj. | 方便的 |

PART ONE　BASIC PART 基础篇

locate	[ləʊˈkeɪt]	v.	定居,位于
option	[ˈɒpʃn]	n.	选择
behavior	[bɪˈheɪvjər]	n.	行为
affordable	[əˈfɔːdəbəl]	adj.	支付得起
local	[ˈləʊkəl]	n.	当地人
be taken for granted			是理所当然的
convenience	[kənˈviːniəns]	n.	方便
respectful etiquettes			礼节

Try to understand

1. Is subway a very important mean of transport around our city?

_____.

2. Do you think it is true or false?

Content	True	False
Sometimes you need to ask for help.		
You don't need to always remember the right exit.		
Buying a subway card is a better option.		
We should always have a good behavior.		

Part D Word Power

Try to collect

Try to understand the meaning of the following description to each line in the

Nanjing Subway and classify them into different station names. Fill in the following form. And if you can, please also try to search more words about subway.

| Line 1: Hongshan Forest Zoo, Xuanwu Lake Park, Xin Jie Kou, The Confucian Temple, Gate of China |
| Line 2: The Memorial Hall of the Victims in Nanjing Massacre by Jap, Nanjing Presidential Palace, The Forbidden City of Nanjing, Zijin Mountain Scenic Area |
| Line 4: Nanjing University, Mount Jiuhua Park |

Lines	Station Names	Useful words and phrases
Line 1		
Line 2		
Line 4		

Part E Language Use

Try to read

1. I'd be happy to help you.

2. Could you tell me how to get to Huqiu?

3. Can you tell me how to use the Ticket Vending Machine in the Nanjing Subway?

4. It departs from Platform 1.

5. By the way, when does it arrive in Suzhou, please?

6. Is this the Inquiry Office?

7. What can I do for you?

8. Take your ticket back, please. Just follow those numbered signs. You can't miss it.

Try to use

Complete the dialogues with the sentences in "try to read":

P: passenger; S: station staff

Dialogue:

P: _____?

S: Yes, it is. _____?

P: Could you tell me from which does the train K181 depart?

S: _____.

P: _____?

S: At 10:22 a.m.

P: Thank you very much.

S: I'd be happy to help you.

Unit 4 Asking the Way and Giving Directions 问路和指路

Learning Objectives

After learning this unit, you should

* Understand the importance of helping others;
* Master how to give out correct directions when the others ask for help;
* Be able to ask the way if necessary.

Advised Hours

2 class hours.

PART ONE BASIC PART 基础篇

Part A Lead-in

Try to think

What places are those in the picture?

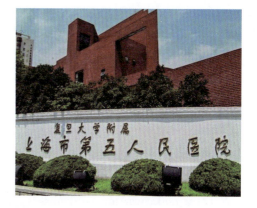

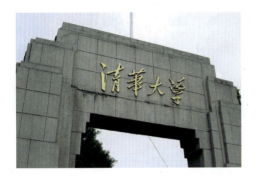

Which places would you like to go and why?

1. Sanya in Hainan Island

2. Terra cotta warriors and horses in Xi'an

3. Jiuzhaigou

4. The Great Wall

5. West Lake

6. Guilin Lijiang River

7. Tibet

8. Taiwan

9. Hong Kong

10. Japan

Part B Dialogue

(Mary is from America. She is at Suzhou Railway Station and is finding his way to Tiger Hill.)

Mary   : Excuse me, Sir?
Volunteer : Yes? Is there anything I can do for you?
Mary   : I want to go to the Tiger Hill. Can you tell me how to get there?
Volunteer : Sure. You can take Subway Line 1, get off at Xiangmen Station and go along the Ganjiang East Road 60 meters, then you can take No. 146 Bus and get off at Huqiu Terminus. You cannot miss it.
Mary   : I beg your pardon? Which station shall I get off first?
Volunteer : Xiangmen Station.
Mary   : Ok, thank you very much.
Volunteer : You are welcome. Have a nice journey.
Mary   : Thanks, bye.

 New Words and Expressions

Suzhou Railway Station	苏州火车站

Ganjiang East Road			干将东路
pardon	[ˈpɑrdn]	v.	抱歉
Xiangmen Station			相门站
Tiger Hill			虎丘
terminus	[ˈtɜːmənəs]	n.	终点站
journey	[ˈdʒɜːnɪ]	n.	旅行,旅程

Part C Passage

Asking for and giving directions with examples

Excuse me, sir. Is there a bank around here?

Yes, there is one right across the street next to library.

Can you give me directions to the petrol station?

Of course I will, just follow this road until you come to the main road. Turn right and then continue for about 100 meters. You will see the petrol station on the left.

Can you tell me how to get to the London Bridge?

I'm sorry I can't help as I'm not native here.

Where's the nearest bus station?

It's on the corner of Oxford Street and Mayfair Lane. Next to the train station.

 New Words and Expressions

library	[ˈlaɪbrerɪ]	n.	图书馆	petrol station		加油站
the London Bridge			伦敦桥	Oxford Street and Mayfair Lane		牛津街和梅菲尔巷

PART ONE　BASIC PART 基础篇

1. If you want to know there is a bank here, what can you say?
   _____.

2. Can you guess the meaning of the word "native"?
   _____.

3. Is the nearest bus station next to the train station?
   _____.

Public places	
Giving directions	

turn right, turn left, on the left, the first crossing, block, avenue, address, across from, corner, next to, nearby, excuse me, go ahead, go along, go straight, be lost, five minutes' walk, China Dinosaur Park, follow... until..., take the No. 330 Bus, take Subway Line 1, I'm new here, I don't know the way around here, beg your pardon, will you kindly tell me, would you please, can you show me

Continue

Asking directions	
Other words	

Part E Language Use

1. ..., but would you please tell me how I can get to Nanjing University?

2. Could you tell me where the convenience store is, please?

3. Well, the store is just on the right.

4. How far is it from Zhujiang Road?

5. It's opposite to the luggage service.

6. Take the escalator and then turn right.

7. ...and interchange at Nanjing Station.

8. Turn right at the second crossing.

Complete the dialogues with the sentences in "try to read":

P: passenger; S: station staff

Dialogue 1:

P: Excuse me, _____?

S: The store, yes. You see the automatic teller machine over there. _____.

P: Thank you.

S: It's a pleasure.

Dialogue 2:

P: Sorry to bother you, _____?

S: Nanjing University, sure. You can take Subway Line 4, _____. Then take Subway Line 1, and get off at Zhujiang Road.

P: Thank you. _____?

S: It's about 5 minutes' walk.

P: Ok, thanks a lot.

Unit 5 Step into the Subway
步入地铁

Learning Objectives

After learning this unit, you should
* Understand some words and logos about subway;
* Master how to introduce the subway service;
* Be able to be friendly and helpful.

Advised Hours

2 class hours.

PART ONE BASIC PART 基础篇

Part A Lead-in

Try to think

What are the logos in China?

Try to discuss

TOP 10 subways in the world

Choose the correct answer:
(The longest/ the busiest/ the most frequently/ the cleanest/ the earliest and

biggest/ the shortest / the deepest/ the cheapest/the fastest/the most convenient)

1. Hong Kong Subway is the _____ in the world.

2. Shanghai Subway is the _____ in the world.

3. Tokyo Subway is the _____ in the world.

4. Singapore Subway is the _____ in the world.

5. Moscow Subway is the _____ in the world.

6. India Subway is the _____ in the world.

7. South Korea Subway is the _____ in the world.

8. Guangzhou Subway is the _____ in the world.

9. Turkey Subway is the _____ in the world.

10. London Subway is the _____ in the world.

Part B Dialogue

(David is from America. He is talking about the Beijing Subway with Mr. Zhang.)

David: Oh, what a beautiful subway station!

Mr. Zhang: Yes. This is Beitucheng Station on Line 10. Welcome to Beijing.

David: It's my great pleasure to take subway today. It's amazing.

Mr. Zhang: This is the new line that is built for the Beijing Daxing International Airport.

David: How many lines are there in the Beijing Subway now?

Mr. Zhang: Altogether 22 lines. And three lines are newly opened last year.

David: Is it convenient to take the subway in Beijing?

Mr. Zhang: I think so. There are so many interchange stations. You only have to choose the shortest route to take.

David: Is the fare distanced-based?

Mr. Zhang: Yes, it is.

David: So it is very important to see the guide sign when I take subway.

Mr. Zhang: Right. You can also ask the staff on the platform. They will help you.

David   : Okay. Thank you very much. Bye.

 New Words and Expressions

amazing	[əˈmeɪzɪŋ]	adj.	令人吃惊的
convenient	[kənˈvinjənt]	adj.	方便的
Beijing Daxing International Airport			北京大兴国际机场
fare	[feə(r)]	n.	车费
staff	[stɑːf]	n.	员工
altogether	[ˌɔltəˈgɛðə]	adv.	总共
choose	[tʃuz]	v.	选择
interchange stations			换乘站
guide sign			标识牌
platform	[ˈplætˌfɔrm]	n.	站台

Part C Passage

Time table of the first & last train of Shanghai Subway Line 1

"EXTENDED" signals the extended time for the last train, and is only shown at night of Friday and Saturday, subject to the station's operation and announcement.

There will be separate arrangement for extended operation on national holidays subject to the condtions of metro stations.

Station	First Train Departure Time			Last Train Departure Time	
	To ShangHai Railway Station ↓	To FuJin Road ↓	To Xin Zhuang ↑	To FuJin Road ↓	To Xin Zhuang ↑
Xinzhuang	5:30		6:04 (Arrive)	22:32 [EXTENDED] 23:50	23:34(Arrive) [EXTENDED] 00:54
Waihuanlu	5:32		6:02	22:34 [EXTENDED] 23:52	23:32 [EXTENDED] 00:52
Lianhua Road	5:34		6:00	22:36 [EXTENDED] 23:54	23:30 [EXTENDED] 00:50
Jinjiang Park	5:37		5:57	22:39 [EXTENDED] 23:57	23:27 [EXTENDED] 00:47
Shanghai South Railway Station	4:55	5:18	5:54	22:42 [EXTENDED] 00:00	23:24 [EXTENDED] 00:44

36

PART ONE   BASIC PART 基础篇

 New Words and Expressions

timetable	[ˈtaɪmteɪbl]	n.	时刻表
subject	[ˈsʌbdʒɪkt]	v.	服从
announcement	[əˈnaʊnsmənt]	n.	通告
arrangement	[əˈrendʒmənt]	n.	安排
extended	[ɪkˈstɛndɪd]	adj.	持续的
departure	[dɪˈpartʃə]	n.	出发,离开
operation	[ˌɑpəˈreʃən]	n.	运行
separate	[ˈsɛpəˌret]	adj.	单独的
national holidays			法定假日

1. Do you think it is true or false?

Content	True	False
Extended signals can be shown at the night of Monday.		
Extended signals are subject to the station's announcement.		
On national holidays there will not be separate arrangements.		
At Shanghai South Railway Station the last train departure time to Fujin Road is 00:00.		

37

2. When was the first and last train departure time in your own city?

Try to guess the meaning of the following words and classify them into different categories. Fill in the following form. And if you can, please try to search more words about subway.

signaling, station, light rail, lift, monorail, guide sign, metro, PSD = platform screen door, AVM = around view monitor, rapid transit, elevated, TVM = ticket vending machine, underground, TO = train operator, AGM = automatic gate machine = around view monitor, SO = station operator, dispatcher, security guard, SSM = shift station master, mechanics, vehicle, air conditioning, power supply, third rail, signal, modern, fast, safe, punctual, convenient and comfortable, crowded and uncomfortable, warm-hearted, careful and friendly

Name for subway	
Job in subway	
Words about subway	

PART ONE BASIC PART 基础篇

	Continue
Other words	

Part E Language Use

Try to read

1. There are many modern machines in subway station.

2. How many lines are there in the Nanjing Subway now?

3. During the rush hour, it is crowded and uncomfortable.

4. Ladies and gentlemen, it's nice to have you aboard our train, and we hope you have a pleasant journey.

5. Your comments and suggestions on our work are always welcome.

6. Our staff members are warm-hearted and careful.

7. What do you think of the Nanjing Metro?

Try to use

Complete the dialogues with the sentences in "try to read":

P: passenger; C: clerk

Dialogue:

P: Good morning. (First time to come to Nanjing)

C: Good morning, welcome to Nanjing.

P: _____?

C: Well, I think it is fast, convenient and comfortable.

39

P: _____?

C: There are 12 lines in Nanjing Subway now.

P: Oh, there are so many lines. I am sure it will be very convenient. Do you think it is crowded?

C: Yes, I think so.

P: Are CCTV and AVM available?

C: Yes, of course.

P: That's great. I see the subway services are always improving.

C: Yes, _____. We are proud of them.

P: Yes, that's wonderful. Thank you, bye.

PART TWO   OPERATIONAL PART
运 营 篇

城市轨道交通专业英语（第2版）

Unit 6 Station Equipment 车站设备

Learning Objectives

After learning this unit, you should

* Understand the function of station platform;
* Master some words about metro station equipment;
* Be able to identify some main station equipment.

Advised Hours

4 class hours.

PART TWO   OPERATIONAL PART 运营篇

Match these pictures with the following words about station equipment.

_____   _____   _____

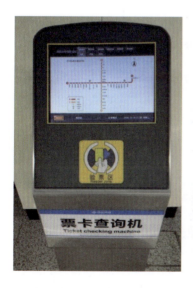

_____   _____   _____

A. Ticket Vending Machine(TVM) B. Ticket Checking Machine(TCM)
C. platform D. Platform Screen Doors(PSD)
E. Automatic Gate Machine (AGM) F. staircase
G. Closed Circuit Television(CCTV) H. elevator
I. escalator

Can you list any other station equipment?

  guide signs; LED display panel; turnstile; trains; route map; line map; concourse.

  sidewalk for the blind; ticket office; moving walkways; emergency escape door...

  (A passenger is taking metro for the first time, he is asking the metro employee for help.)

PART TWO OPERATIONAL PART 运营篇

P = passenger; M = metro employee

P: Excuse me, it's my first time to take subway in Nanjing. There are so much high-tech facilities at the metro station that I'm puzzled. Would you please be so kind to tell me what they are?

M: Of course. Metro transportation has developed rapidly during the past few years. I'm sure you will have an unforgettable experience here. Now we are in Xinjiekou Station on Line 1.

P: Oh, I see. What's that? Many people are queuing there.

M: That is ticket vending machine. People can buy tickets on the machine by themselves.

P: And how can I go through the gate and enter the station?

M: Let me show you. Put your ticket here and then the door will open after "beep" sound, go through the door you'll get in the metro station.

P: How convenient it is! Now we're arriving at concourse. Look, how bright it is!

M: Be cautious not to cross the yellow line when you're waiting for the train.

P: Thanks for your reminding.

M: It's my pleasure.

New Words and Expressions

high-tech	[ˈhaitek]	adj.	高科技的
transportation	[ˌtrænspɔːˈteiʃən]	n.	交通运输

concourse	[ˈkɒŋkɔːs]	n.	站厅
facility	[fəˈsiliti]	n.	设备
unforgettable	[ˌʌnfəˈgetəbl]	adj.	令人难忘的
experience	[ɪkˈspɪərɪəns]	n.	经验；经历
queue	[kjuː]	v.	排队
cautious	[ˈkɔːʃəs]	adj.	谨慎的

Metro platform

A metro platform is a section of pathway, alongside rail tracks at a metro station, at which passengers may board or alight from trains. It is a feature of station design on metro railways throughout the world that platforms are built to the height of the train floor, or close to it.

Some metro stations have platform screen doors between the platforms and the tracks. They provide more safety, and they allow the heating or air conditioning in the station to be separated from the ventilation in the tunnel, thus being more efficient and effective.

Platform width is also an important feature of station design. The width must be sufficient to accommodate the largest numbers of passengers expected but must not be wasteful of space. Ideally platforms should be straight or slightly convex, so that the guard can see the whole train when preparing to close the doors. Also passenger carriages are straight, so doors will not always open directly onto a curved platform—often a platform gap is present.

Usually such platforms will have warning signs, possibly auditory, such as London Underground's famous phrase "Mind the gap". Columns supporting structures can often seriously affect the operation of a station by reducing circulating areas and passenger flows at busy times. Platform edges should be straight to assist operations by allowing clear sight lines.

1. What is the function of metro platform?
   _____.

2. What is the feature of station design on metro railways throughout the world?
   _____.

3. What is the disadvantage of the columns supporting structure in the metro station?
   _____.

Classify the following words and phrases into different categories.

track, third rail, live rail, newsagent, elevator, guide signs, ATM, AVM, tunnel, convenience stores, escalator, electronic timetable display, fire equipment cabinets, fire alarm system, power supply system, telecommunication system, signal system, ticket office

Equipment for tickets	

Continue

Equipment at the concourse	
Equipment for station systems	
Equipment for subway vehicles	
Others	

1. You can buy it through the machine.

2. You can recharge your card through the machine or at the Customer Service Centre.

3. You can require it through the Ticket Checking Machine over there.

4. Here are your ticket and change.

5. Sorry for the inconvenience.

6. Maybe there's something wrong with the machine.

7. Please change for RMB at the bank.

Complete the dialogues with the sentences in "try to read":

P: passenger; S: station staff

Dialogue 1:

P: Excuse me, where can I get a ticket?

S: _____. It's over there.

P: Can I pay with US dollars?

S: Sorry, we don't accept foreign currency. _____.

Dialogue 2:

P: Please tell me why the ticket doesn't come out.

S: _____. Don't worry. Let me check it for you. Please wait a moment.

(A few minutes later)

S: The machine is OK now. _____. _____.

P: That's all right.

Unit 7 Station Service

车站服务

Learning Objectives

After learning this unit, you should

* Understand the responsibilities as a metro employee;
* Master some words and phrases about station service;
* Be able to serve passengers in English and deal with common problems.

Advised Hours

4 class hours.

PART TWO OPERATIONAL PART 运营篇

Part A Lead-in

Have you ever taken subway? Can you put the following steps in order?

(　　) Wait for the train

(　　) Get on and enjoy the ride

(　　) Get off

(　　) Swipe card and go through the turnstile

(　　) Exit

(　　) Buy a ticket of token

How do you deal with these occasions, if you were a metro employee?

1. If a disabled man in a wheelchair wants to take the subway, _____
_____.

2. If a passenger's card is invalid, _____.

3. If a passenger can't find the way to exit, _____.

Part B Dialogue

(*A metro employee is serving a passenger whose destination is Hehai University.*)

P = passenger; M = metro employee

P: Excuse me, I'd like to go to Hehai University. Which line should I take?

M: You can take Line 1 first, and then change to Line S1.

P: Where can I change to Line S1?

M: You can change at Nanjing South Station. It's a transfer station.

P: Thank you very much. But my metro card is broken. Where can I get it replaced?

M: Sorry. We can't replace your card here. You can also replace it at the transfer station-Nanjing South Station.

P: Can I have the value of the card refunded?

M: If the card is damaged, the value of the card cannot be refunded.

P: What about the balance on my current card?

M: The balance of your current card will be transferred to your new card.

P: OK, thanks a lot.

M: It's my pleasure.

New Words and Expressions

| university | [ˌjuːniˈvəːsiti] | n. | 大学 |

transfer	[ˈtrænsfə]	v.	换车；转移
replace	[riˈpleis]	v.	更换
damage	[ˈdæmidʒ]	v.	损坏
value	[ˈvæljuː]	n.	价值
refund	[riːˈfʌnd]	v.	退还
balance	[ˈbæləns]	n.	余额
current	[ˈkʌrənt]	adj.	现在的

Metro radio

Dear passengers, welcome to take Nanjing Metro Train. There are TVMs at both sides of the station hall. Please queue up at the TVM to buy the single tickets. If you want to buy the stored-value tickets or recharge your tickets, please go to the ticket office or information desk. Children above 1.1 m should buy a ticket to enter the station.

You can take the train with single tickets or stored-value tickets. The single tickets can only be used on the day of purchasing and at the station where you buy the ticket, or it is invalid. Each stored-value ticket can only be used by one person each time. If you fail to exit the station within 120 minutes, an extra fee of the highest ticket price will be charged when you exit. If you have any questions about the ticket, please ask the ticket office or information desk for help. Thanks for your cooperation.

Passengers for departure, please exit the station at the guidance of the station signs. Please queue up and put the tickets into the recycling tanks. The single tickets are recycled and the stored-value tickets shall be taken care of. If there is something wrong with the ticket, please ask the ticket office or the information for help. Thank you for your cooperation.

Try to understand

1. According to the passage, who can take metro for free?

 .

2. If I bought a single ticket at Xinjiekou Station, will it be still valid next day? Why?

 .

3. If I can't exit the station within two hours, must I pay any extra fee? If so, how much should I pay?

 .

4. How can you deal with the single-ride ticket and stored-value ticket when you leave the station?

 .

Try to collect

Classify the following words into different categories.

departure, stairs, escalator, elevator/lift, cargo lift, ATM, drinking water, service & complaints hotline, information, fire hydrant, emergency alarm, seats reserved for seniors, children, pregnant women, the sick and the disabled, first/last train from this station, map of ×××station, map of ××× area, ticket office, machine out of order, please go to the nearest station to buy or recharge IC cards, swipe your card here, automatic ticket machine/ ticket vending machine, IC card inquiry service, fare adjustment

PART TWO OPERATIONAL PART 运营篇

broadcasting	
facilities	
other service	

Part E Language Use

Try to read

1. How often does the train run?
2. How many stops from here?
3. How long should it take?
4. Please follow the arrow in the passage.
5. Sorry to keep you waiting.
6. There's a passageway for disabled people. I'll take you there.
7. We can return the fare.
8. You can change to another transport.

Try to use

Complete the dialogue with the sentences in "try to read":

P: passenger; S: station staff

Dialogue:

S: Where are you going?

P: Guanghuiqiao. _____?

S: Three.

P: _____?

S: It looks like 7 minutes. Please wait a moment.

P: _____?

S: Every 10 minutes.

(A while later)

P: What's the matter? Why hasn't the train arrived yet?

S: _____. There must be something wrong. Please wait patiently. If you are in a hurry. _____.

P: How about my ticket?

S: _____.

PART TWO   OPERATIONAL PART 运营篇

 **Tickets**

票务

Learning Objectives

After learning this unit, you should
* Understand some ticket rules and policies;
* Master some words and expressions related to tickets;
* Be able to provide passengers with ticket service.

Advised Hours

4 class hours.

Part A Lead-in

Identify the pictures. Match them with the words below.

A. irregular-shaped cards   B. single-ride ticket
C. public transportation card   D. one-day ticket
E. Automatic Gate Machine   F. Ticket Vending machine
G. tourist souvenir ticket   H. route map
I. Automatic Teller Machine

Which payment method is most widely used in your cities? Why?

cash

Alipay

union pay

wechat pay

(*In the ticket office, a passenger is consulting the metro employee.*)

P = passenger; M = metro employee

P: Excuse me. There must be something wrong with my ticket. I put it in the magnetic area, but there is not any respond, I can't go through the door.

M: Let me check it for you. Your single ticket was purchased yesterday, and it's invalid today. You must buy another one.

P: Oh, it's so inconvenient. Can I get a metro card now?

M: Sure. You can apply for a stored-value card which is also called money-inside ticket of "one card through the city". There is a 20 RMB deposit, and a 20 RMB minimum for your first charge.

P: Here's 100 RMB, I want to put 80 RMB on the card.

M: 20 for the deposit, 80 for the card, 100 in total. This is your new card and receipt.

P: Thanks. By the way, I want to know whether I can have my card back if I lose it.

M: There is no record of the cards. So if you lose it, you'll just have to get a new one.

P: I see. Thank you.

M: It's my pleasure.

 New Words and Expressions

consult	[kən'sʌlt]	v.	咨询
magnetic	[mæg'netik]	adj.	有磁性的
purchase	['pəːtʃəs]	v.	购买
invalid	[in'vælid]	adj.	无效的
inconvenient	[ˌinkən'viːnjənt]	adj.	不方便的
apply for			办理

stored-value card			储值卡
deposit	[diˈpɔzit]	n.	押金
receipt	[riˈsiːt]	n.	收据

Part C Passage

Ticket Types

1) One-way ticket

One-way tickets can only be used on the day of purchasing and at the station the passenger buy the ticket, or it is invalid. The loss can't be reported. Passengers taking the one-way tickets must make fare adjustment when it's over regular journey or time.

2) Anniversary ticket

The tickets are issued only for some major festivals or commemorative activities according to certain plans. There are special rules for the use of the tickets each time they are issued. Anniversary tickets are non-returnable. The money in tickets should be used up within the prescribed periods and the ticket is not recycled, and the loss can't be reported.

3) The fixed counted time tickets

The tickets are issued with limited frequency of use, and they will be used within the periods of validity. The tickets are not recycled and refundable, and the loss can't be reported.

Ticket Discount Policy

1) The student card

It's a discount card for students, and passengers can enjoy 50 percent concessions on one-way ticket fare.

2) The cards free of charge

They are free cards for the aged over 70 years old, the disabled soldiers, the disabled police due to public, the blind, Grade 1 or 2 disabled people. They must have valid documents for free cards. Grade 3 or 4 disabled people can have the half price

AIXIN cards, and the necessary auxiliary appliances carried by the disabled people should be free.

3) One adult passenger can take a child under the height of 1.2 meters (including 1.2 meters) for free, and if there is more than one child, the other child should buy a ticket.

1. Can you recharge the anniversary tickets? Why?

_____.

2. Can the money in the fixed counted time tickets be transferred to a new card? Why?

_____.

3. Which kinds of passengers can take metro for free?

_____.

Classify the following words into different categories.

vend, collect, count, automatize, traffic card, statistics, data, non-contact, ticket media, magnetic card, smart card, one-way ticket, anniversary ticket, fixed counted time tickets, valid time of ticket, money-inside ticket, 1 ticket just for 1 person, children higher than 1.2 meters need to purchase full price ticket, one adult passenger can take a child under the height of 1.2 meters for free, students can enjoy 50 percent concessions on one-way ticket fare, one-way ticket can't be refunded once sold	
Definition of AFC	
Ticket media	
Ticket rules	

Part E Language Use

Try to read

1. How much is the ticket? What's the fare?

2. I need a transfer.

3. It's a one-price ticket.

4. I can change for you.

5. Please buy your ticket before going in.

6. Please keep your magnetic ticket for exit.

7. Please go to the ticket office for help.

8. Children above 1.2 meters should buy a ticket.

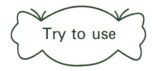

Complete the dialogue with the sentences in "try to read":

P: passenger; S: station staff

Dialogue:

P: I'm going to take the subway. _____?

S: Two yuan for a ticket. _____.

P: _____.

S: All the same. By the way, do you have coins?

P: No.

S: OK, _____. Wait a moment, please. Here's your change. Here you are.

P: By the way, does my boy need to buy a ticket?

S: Yes, he does because his height is above 1.2 meters. _____.

PART TWO   OPERATIONAL PART 运营篇

Unit 9 Broadcasting

地铁广播

Learning Objectives

After learning this unit, you should

* Understand the necessities of metro broadcasting;
* Master main expressions and sentences about broadcasting;
* Be able to broadcast when needed.

Advised Hours

6 class hours.

Part A Lead-in

Try to think

How can we get information from metro station? Try to read and match.

A. the information   B. volunteer   C. guide signs
D. metro staff   E. broadcasting

Try to discuss

What kind of announcement have you heard at metro station or on the train?

1. Metro station regulations and service.

2. Real-time information broadcasting.

3. Information promoting broadcasting.

4. Lost and found.

(*Xiao Wang, as an intern at a metro company, is on broadcasting duty. Now he is turning to his colleague, Mr. Chen for some advice.*)

Xiao Wang: Good morning, Mr. Chen. Would you please do me a favor?

Mr. Chen: Certainly. What's the matter?

Xiao Wang: I will work as an intern on broadcasting position in the short future. But I'm not sure about using some broadcasting terms. I wonder if you could help me.

Mr. Chen: No problem. And what kind of terms do you refer to?

Xiao Wang: If there are too many people on the station, what shall I do to remind passengers?

Mr. Chen: In that case, you should broadcast as "Your attention, please! Crowd Management Plans are now in operation. Please don't wait inside the station. Follow directions to exit. Thank you for your cooperation."

Xiao Wang: Oh, I see. And to keep a good order, what kind of announcement shall I broadcast?

Mr. Chen: Broadcast as, "Your attention, please! For safety reasons, please use the lift if you have baggage or bulky items. Please let passengers exit first and keep clear from the screen door. Thank you for your cooperation."

Xiao Wang: One more question, how can I deal with emergency broadcasting?

Mr. Chen: "Your attention please! This is an emergency. Please leave the station immediately." or "Your attention please. This is an emergency. Please follow directions and leave the station immediately.

Remain calm. Don't run."

Xiao Wang: I really appreciate your pronunciation. Thanks a lot.

Mr. Chen: My pleasure.

 New Words and Expressions

broadcast	[ˈbrɔːdkɑːst]	v.	广播
do me a favor			帮我个忙
passenger	[ˈpæsindʒə]	n.	乘客
attention	[əˈtenʃən]	n.	注意
announcement	[əˈnaunsmənt]	n.	通知
baggage	[ˈbægidʒ]	n.	行李
bulky	[ˈbʌlki]	adj.	笨重的
emergency	[iˈməːdʒənsi]	n.	紧急情况
remain calm			保持冷静
pronunciation	[prəˌnʌnsiˈeiʃən]	n.	发音

PART TWO   OPERATIONAL PART 运营篇

Part C Passage

Metro broadcasting

1. Your attention please! Crowd Management Plans are now in operation and some of the entry gates are temporarily shut down. They will be back in use in a few minutes. Please accept our apologies for any inconvenience or delay this might cause.

2. Your attention please! Please follow staff directions to enter as the entry gates are not working. We apologize for any inconvenience this might cause.

3. Your attention please! Inflammable, explosive or poisonous items are strictly prohibited anywhere in the system. Thank you for your cooperation.

4. Dear passengers, please stand at the right side of the escalator, and leave the left side open for traffic.

5. When using the escalators, stands firm, holds the handrail. Please don't run or walk in the wrong direction. Thank you!

6. For safety reasons, please use the lift if you have baggage or bulky item. Thank you!

7. Please wait for the train behind the yellow line on the platform.

8. The train is arriving. Please mind the gap between the train and the platform.

9. Please wait in line while passengers exit from the train. Down first, later on. Thank you!

10. If you're traveling a distance, please move further inside the train, thank you!

11. Please do not lean or put hands on the doors.

12. Please take care of your children and belongings. Thank you!

13. Ladies and gentlemen, welcome to Nanjing MTR, wish you have a pleasant journey!

14. To keep a clean and healthy environment, don't smoke or litter in trains and stations. Please offer your seats to anyone in need. Thank you for your cooperation!

15. For keeping equipment and facilities have good functions, please be consider-

ate when you use that, thanks for your cooperation.

16. Ladies and gentlemen, you are taking a green smoking-free train, it equips smoking detector. For your and others' travelling safety, please don't smoke within any area on the train.

17. The next stop is Nanjing South Station, you can transfer the metro Line 1, Line S1 and Line S3. Please get ready to Exit, from the left side.

18. Ladies and gentlemen, we are approaching Confucius Temple Station, please check your luggage and prepare to get off the train.

19. Your attention, please! There will be a short delay before the doors open. Please stand back from the platform screen doors. Thanks for your cooperation.

20. Please alight front door of this carriage, the door on the left side will be used.

21. Ladies and gentlemen, we are now at Nanjing Forestry University Station. Please take all your belongings and get off the train from the doors on the left.

22. Please have your ticket ready before you reach the exit gate. Thank you!

23. Your attention please! This is an emergency. Please follow directions and leave immediately.

24. Your attention please! The last train for Nanjing South Station departs at 11:10. Please board immediately.

25. Your attention please! Train service for today has ended. Please leave the station. Thank you.

Try to understand

Read the following statements and tell T (true) or F (false).

1. (   ) The passenger can take gasoline on the train.

2. (   ) Only the disabled people can use the lift.

3. (   ) The passenger should follow the principle "On first, later down".

4. (   ) While waiting for a train, passengers can stand anywhere on the platform.

5. (   ) When using the escalators, passengers shall stand at the left side, in order

to leave the right open for traffic.

Classify the following words and phrases into different categories.

Line 1, Airport Line, All Metro Lines, Exit A, of a technical fault on a train, someone is on a track, of a fire in tunnel, of a derailment, of a problem with the power supply, of a signaling fault, of a train collision, platform screen doors have failed, of flooding, both ends of the concourse, both ends of the platform, the emergency exit, Nanjing South station, Confucius Temple, Nanjing Forestry University, Olympic Sports Centre	
Line	
Station	
Location	

	Continue
Exit	
Emergency	

Part E Language Use

1. Crowd Management Plans are now in operation.
2. Follow directions to exit.
3. For safety reasons, please use the lift if you have baggage or bulky items.
4. Thank you for your cooperation.
5. Some of the entry gates are temporarily shut down.
6. And keep clear from the screen door.
7. Please don't wait inside the station.
8. Please let passengers exit first.

Complete the dialogues with the sentences in "try to read":

PART TWO OPERATIONAL PART 运营篇

L: Li Ping; H: Han Dong

Dialogue:

L: Hi, Han Dong. I wonder if you could help me?

H: Sure, what's the matter?

L: I will work as an intern on broadcasting position in the short future. But how can I broadcast correctly? I'm not sure about using broadcasting items. I wonder if you could help me with this.

H: No problem. And what kind of terms do you refer to?

L: If there are too many people on the station, what shall I do to remind passengers?

H: In that case, you should broadcast like this "Your attention, please! _____. _____. _____. _____. We apologize for any inconvenience this might cause."

L: And how can I broadcast to keep order?

H: " Your attention please! _____. _____. _____. _____."

L: Your English pronunciation is really good. Thanks a lot.

H: That's all right.

Unit 10 Security

安全运营

Learning Objectives

After learning this unit, you should

* Understand the importance of metro security check;
* Master words and expressions about security signs and devices;
* Be able to know how to have security check for passengers.

Advised Hours

4 class hours.

Part A Lead-in

Here is some commonly used equipment that ensures security. Try to match each device with the following words.

_____   _____   _____

_____   _____   _____

A. walk-through metal detector B. handheld metal detector

C. security guard D. Portable Raman detector

E. X-ray security equipment F. CCTV

Try to discuss

Name the following signs in English. Can you tell more safety signs?

(*A passenger is accepting security check at metro station.*)

P = passenger; S = security guard

S: Excuse me sir! Would you please put your carry-on baggage on the belt?

P: OK, just a moment... Alright, there you go.

S: Hmm... the X-ray machine is showing some strange things in your bag. I'll have to search it.

P: Sure, go ahead. I don't have any dangerous items on me.

S: Sir! Have these bags been in your possession at all times?

P: Yes, I've had them in my sight since I packed them.

S: I see... And what is this? You didn't think you could get on the train with such a dangerous item, did you?

P: It's just a bottle of perfume.

S: It is strictly prohibited to take the train with any inflammable, explosive items.

P: Well, alright... I didn't realize perfume is inflammable.

S: Do you have any other dangerous items in your carry-on bags?

P: I don't think so.

S: Alright, I've finished searching your belongings. You can go now.

P: Thanks.

New Words and Expressions

carry-on baggage			随身行李
search	[sə:tʃ]	v.	搜查
possession	[pəˈzeʃən]	n.	个人财物
have... in sight			使…在视线范围内
pack	[pæk]	v.	打包
perfume	[ˈpə:fju:m]	n.	香水
inflammable	[inˈflæməbl]	adj.	易燃的
explosive	[iksˈpləusiv]	adj.	易爆的

Guangzhou tightens metro security check

Guangzhou Metro has upgraded the level of security check. The new metro security measure comes as Guangzhou, an international country, is facing more severe challenges of violent terrorist attacks. A terrorist bombing attack occurred at an open air market in Urumqi, capital of far west China's Xinjiang Uygur Autonomous Region, on May 22,2014, leaving 39 people dead and 94 others injured. That followed a string of violent attacks that shocked the country, including one at a train station in the southwestern city of Kunming On March 1,2014, and another one at Tian'anmen Square in Beijing on October 28,2014.

Guangzhou Metro indicated that a total of 6 X-ray inspection instruments have been used in certain stations from November 14,2015, including two at Guangzhou Railway Station, one at Gongyuanqian Station, one at Tiyu Xilu Station, one at Zumiao Station, and one at Kuiqi Lu Station. Earlier on September 25 in this year, Guangzhou Metro has set up checkpoints in all stations security. Every station has equipment for detecting explosive and all security staff are equipped metal and liquid detectors.

The new security procedures will require both passengers and their baggage to undergo an X-ray scanner, much the same as airport security. Although Guangzhou Metro indicated that upgrading the level of security check will not waste too much time for passengers to enter the station, people who get on the trains in those stations may set off a little earlier than before, in case of the long queue.

1. Why does Guangzhou subway tighten the security check?

2. How many X-ray inspection instruments are added? In which stations?

3. Why shall passengers set off earlier than before?

Classify the following words and phrases into different categories.

don't climb on the lift truck, stand clear of the platform, detonator, no admittance, speak microphone alarm, turn handle counterclockwise 90 degrees, don't touch, temporarily closed, sand bucket, explosion proof tank, please exit in order, firecrackers, don't block access, don't distract the driver, press button in emergency, stay clear from tracks, fire extinguisher, fire hydrant, gasoline, painting, liquefied gas

Security signs	
Security objects	
Dangerous items	

1. Would you please go through the security check?

2. Would you please open your bag? I'm afraid there's something suspicious in your bag.

3. For the safety of passenger, you can't smoke here.

4. It will only take you a minute or two.

5. Security check is to ensure the safety of the subway and all passengers.

6. Every passenger has to go through security check.

7. Just put your backpack on the belt through the X-ray scanner.

8. Would you please move away from the connecting gangway?

9. Please don't throw anything out of the window.

10. Hands off the doorframe.

Complete the dialogues with the sentences in "try to read":

A metro employee is persuading some passengers to obey metro security regulations.

P: passenger; M: metro employee

Dialogue:

(at the entry)

M: Excuse me, miss. _____?

P: Is it necessary? There's nothing dangerous in my backpack.

M: Miss, _____. _____. This regulation is binding on everybody.

P: But I'm in a hurry to work. I don't have enough time for the security check.

M: Miss, _____. It's very convenient. _____.

P: Ok.

M: Thanks for your cooperation.

(In the cabin)

M: Excuse me, sir, but smoking is not allowed in the cabin.

P1: Oh. I'm sorry, I didn't know. Is smoking forbidden here?

M: Yes. _____. It's a major cause of fires. You can go between the cars. There's an ashtray on the wall, and you can smoke there.

P1: Thank you.

M: Excuse me. _____. It may possibly hit someone passing by.

P2: Sorry. I see.

M: Look out, madam. _____. Otherwise your fingers may get pinched at any time.

P3: Oh, thank you for your concern.

M: _____? It's dangerous to stay here.

P4: Thank you very much. I'm leaving now.

PART THREE   FACILITIES PART
设 施 篇

Unit 11 Definition of the Metro System
地铁系统定义

Learning Objectives

After learning this unit, you should
* Understand some vocabulary about metro system;
* Master classification of metro systems;
* Be able to introduce the metro system.

Advised Hours

4 class hours.

PART THREE   FACILITIES PART 设施篇

How many cities facilitated metro system in our country?

1. What is "underground railway"?
2. Metro systems are classified into _____.

A: What is ATO?
B: It is Automatic Train Operation.
A: What is the main function of ATO?
B: It ensures the normal running and optimizing of train dispatch and strengths acceleration, instead of traditional model of Trains' operation. For example, one of leading functions is to monitor and control door opening system.
A: What is the significant advantage?
B: It can reduce human operation errors and potential risks it may cause.
A: Is ATO applied in China?
B: Yes, it is more widely applied in China and developed rapidly, both integrated system and inside decorations, the capacity is much higher than developed countries even.

New Words and Expressions

ATO	Automatic Train Operation	n.	列车自动运行系统
function	[fʌŋkʃən]	n.	功能
accelerate	[ækˈseləreit]	vt.	使增速
applied	[əˈplaɪd]	adj.	应用的
optimize	[ɔptimaiz]	vt.	使最优化
error	[ˈerə(r)]	n.	过失,失误

Part C Passage

1. Definition and description of the metro system

The metro, or sometimes named as "underground railway", is a transportation system which exclusively uses electric traction and usually uses the traditional steel wheels (sometimes rubber-tyred wheels). With rail guidance system on an exclusive corridor, the largest part of which is underground and could be grade separated from the rest of the urban road and pedestrian traffic.

The system of other modes that urban transport related is characterized by high-frequency service (train headway up to 1 min) and large capacity (up to 45,000 passengers direction) movement. To a large percentage or the entire length on an underground exclusive corridor, high construction cost (€60-130 m/track-km or even higher in some cases), long implementation period (in some cases even decades), from an engineering point of view, it is a very complex and challenging project, as it requires specialized knowledge regarding a variety of engineering disciplines (soil mechanics, structural mechanics, transportation engineering, architecture, power supply systems, low-voltage telecommunication systems, track work technologies, automated control systems, rolling stock technologies, computer systems, etc.)

2. Classification of metro systems

Based on the passenger volume loading, metro systems shall be classified into heavy metro and light metro.

The light metro is a hybrid, solution between the heavy metro and tramway. Compared with the heavy metro, the light metro is characterized by lower transport capacity, lighter vehicles and shorter distance between intermediate stops. It is commonly and popularly selected as the leading transport for the cities, which inhabitant population less than one million. On the other hand, the construction of heavy metro is more appropriate for cities with inhabitant population greater than one million.

3. Automation grade of train operation

Based on the Grade of Automation (GOA) of train operation, metro systems are classified into four categories.

More specifics:

GOA1: Operation with a driver. The driver of the train is actively involved throughout the driving activity. The train is only equipped with Automatic Train Protection (ATP) system.

GOA2: Semi-automatic Train Operation (STO). The train is equipped with ATP and Automatic Train Operation (ATO) systems. However, only in situation of system failure, the supervising driver undertakes driving duty, i.e. be responsible for door opening and closing only.

GOA3: Driverless Train Operation. The train moves without a driver. An on duty attendant standing by is responsible for the door opening and closing, and can intervene train operation in case of system failure. Besides, the train is equipped with both ATP and ATO systems.

GOA4: Unattended Train Operation. Equipped with ATP and ATO systems, the train moves automatically and all of the above operations are performed without the presence of a driver or an attendant.

In General, the train operation is deemed as automatic when the trains are driverless (GOA4 and GOA3). These two GOAs must be facilitated with automatic sliding gates along the platforms (Platform Screen Doors, PSD) to guarantee passenger safety.

New Words and Expressions

corridor	[ˈkɔːrɪdɔːr]	n.	走廊;过道;通道
pedestrian	[pəˈdestrɪən]	n.	人行道
frequency	[ˈfriːkwənsi]	n.	频率
capacity	[kəˈpæsəti]	n.	容量;容积;容纳能力
discipline	[ˈdɪsəplɪnz]	n.	训练方法;行为准则;符合准则的行为
telecommunication	[ˌtelɪkəˌmjuːnɪˈkeɪʃn]	n.	电信
appropriate	[əˈprəʊprieɪt]	adj.	合适的,适宜的
intervene	[ˌɪntəˈviːn]	v.	阻碍;干扰;介入
equipped with	装备,设置	be facilitated with	配备,设置,安装
separated from	分离;把……和……分开	classified into	被分类为
appropriate for	合适	compared with	与……相比

1. What is characterized of the light metro?

2. What is GOA?

PART THREE　FACILITIES PART 设施篇

Try to collect

What is ATP? _____ .
What is STO? _____ .
What is ATO? _____ .
What is PSD? _____ .

Try to read

1. fixed-point stopping　定点停车
2. automatic train control　列车自动控制
3. automatic train supervision　列车自动监控
4. automatic train protection　列车自动防护
5. automatic train operation　列车自动运行
6. driverless train control　无人驾驶

1. What is automatictrain control?
_____ .

2. What is driverless train control?
_____ .

Unit 12 Third Rail of a Metro System
地铁系统轨道

Learning Objectives

After learning this unit, you should
* Understand some vocabularies about third-rail;
* Master the benefits and disadvantages of third-rail systems;
* Be able to introduce third rail.

Advised Hours

4 class hours.

PART THREE FACILITIES PART 设施篇

What kind of rail have you seen?

Why have different rails of metro system?

A: Could you please introduce the track superstructure? I mean the topside of the track.

B: Well, the track superstructure is usually made of concrete slab.

A: Why does this track bed system is applied, instead of the ballasted track?

B: Because it's easier to maintain and its annual maintenance cost much lower.

A: Any other factors?

B: Compared with others, current proposal lasts longer time and is more applicable to local climates in technical aspect. As we know, in China, the system has been widely facilitated more than 30 provinces. It may cover variety of geographical environments, technical team need to consider of engineering works in different types of terrains, such as rocky land, farm land, river, valley, mountain, dessert...

A: That's true. In fact, it's quiet complicated. Except the cost, the key point is technical parts, we can't ignore the role of engineering and maintenance. Four seasons a year is also a big challenge.

B: Now I see, it's only just the cost matter.

New Words and Expressions

concrete	[ˈkɒŋkriːt]	adj.	混凝土制的
maintenance	[ˈmeɪntənəns]	n.	保养；维护；维持
factor	[ˈfæktər]	n.	因素，要素
climate	[ˈklaɪmət]	n.	气候，气候区
geographical	[ˌdʒiːəˈgræfɪkl]	adj.	地理的
engineering	[ˌendʒɪˈnɪrɪŋ]	n.	工程；工程学；设计制造
terrain	[təˈreɪn]	n.	地形；地势；地带
valley	[ˈvæli]	n.	谷；山谷；溪谷；流域
complicated	[ˈkɒmplɪkeɪtɪd]	adj.	复杂的
ignore	[ɪgˈnɔː(r)]	v.	忽视；对……不予理会
rocky land			多岩石地带
variety of			各种各样的

Part C Passage

Third-rail at the West Falls Church Metro stop near Washington, D. C., electrified at 750 volts. The third-rail is at the follow of the figure, with a white canopy above it. The two lower rails are the ordinary running rails; current from the third-rail returns to the power station through these.

PART THREE FACILITIES PART 设施篇

A British Class 442 third-rail electric multiple unit in Dorset is the fastest class of third-rail EMU in the world, reaching 108 mph(173 km/h).

Paris Metro's guiding rails of the rubber-tyred lines are also current conductors. The current collector is between the pair of rubber wheels.

A third-rail is a method of providing electric power to a railway train, through a continuous rigid conductor placed alongside or between the rails of a railway track. It is used typically in a mass transit or rapid transit system, which has alignments in its own corridors, fully or almost fully segregated from the outside environment. In most cases, third-rail systems supply direct current electricity.

The third-rail system of electrification is unrelated to the third-rail used in dual-gauge railways.

Third rail systems are a means of providing electric traction power to railway trains, and they use an additional rail (called a "conductor rail") for the purpose. On most systems, the conductor rail is placed on the sleeper ends outside the running rails, but in some cases a central conductor rail is used. The conductor rail is supported on ceramic insulators or insulated brackets, typically at intervals of 10 feet (3 meters) or so.

The trains have metal contact blocks called "shoes" which make contact with the conductor rail. The traction current is returned to the generating station through the running rails. The conductor rail is usually made of high conductivity steel, and the running rails have to be electrically connected using wire bonds or other devices, to minimize resistance in the electric circuit.

The conductor rails have to be interrupted at level crossings and at crossovers, and ramps are provided at the ends of the sections to give a smooth transition to the train shoes.

There is considerable diversity about the contact position between the train and the rail; some of the earliest systems used top contact, but developments used side or bottom contact, which enabled the conductor rail to be covered, protecting track workers from accidental contact and protecting the conductor rail from snow and leaf fall.

Benefits and disadvantages of third-rail systems

Electric traction systems (where electric power is generated at a remote power station and transmitted to the trains) are considerably more cost-effective than diesel or steam units, where the power unit is carried on the train. This advantage is especially marked in urban and rapid transit systems with a high traffic density.

So far as first cost is concerned, third-rail systems are relatively cheap to install, compared to overhead wire contact systems, as no structures for carrying the overhead contact wires are required, and there is no need to reconstruct over bridges to provide clearances. There is much less visual intrusion on the environment.

New Words and Expressions

multiple	[ˈmʌltɪpl]	adj. n.	多重的；多样的；许多的 倍数；[电] 并联
current	[ˈkɜːrənt]	adj. n.	现在的；流通的 （水，气，电）流；趋势；涌流

PART THREE　FACILITIES PART 设施篇

conductor	[kənˈdʌktər]	n.	导体;售票员
electrification	[ɪˌlektrɪfɪˈkeɪʃn]	n.	电气化;带电;充电
insulate	[ˈɪnsəleɪt]	vt.	隔离,使孤立;使绝缘,使隔热
interval	[ˈɪntərvl]	n.	间隔;间距
ramp	[ræmp]	n.	斜坡,坡道;敲诈
considerable	[kənˈsɪdərəbl]	adj.	相当大的;重要的,值得考虑的
diversity	[daɪˈvɜːrsəti]	n.	多样性;差异
be provided at			提供在

1. What is "shoes" in part C?

2. Talk about benefits and disadvantages of third-rail systems?

Do you know anything about rail? Please write them down.

95

Part E Language Use

1. examine and repair period   检修周期
2. track   轨道
3. track gauge   轨距
4. track fastening   扣件
5. sleeper   轨枕
6. turnout/switch   道岔

1. What is examine and repair period?

2. What is function of the turnout?

PART THREE　　FACILITIES PART 设施篇

Unit 13　Metro Stations

地铁站

Learning Objectives

After learning this unit, you should

* Understand some vocabularies about metro stations;
* Master the functions of metro stations;
* Be able to introduce metro stations.

Advised Hours

4 class hours.

Part A Lead-in

What kind of metro station do you like?

What are the functions of metro station?

Part B Dialogue

A: Is there any security check in Nanjing?

B: Yes, absolutely at the entry of the metro, full set of security checking equipment operation 24 hour, under duty staff governor. All passengers will be requested to leave their belongings on rolling-checking board before enter metro platform.

A: All belongings? Small and big bags too?

B: Yeah, big and small bags, shopping bags, luggage... whatever.

A: It sounds like... trouble passengers. Is it really necessary? I don't think it's convenient.

B: Well, hmm... All rule is for public safety. Sometimes security will ask passenger to open the bottle and drink a bit before entry.

A: But must be some other certain ways is optional to prevent accidents, right?

B: Sure, some safety signs have been posted along the exit and entry of metro.

A: I see, for public safety, the more contributions the better, never complain the facilities.

B: The sign in subway is really very important and helpful. It helps a lot, especially to people running in a hurry.

A: Exactly.

 New Words and Expressions

security	[sɪˈkjʊrəti]	n. adj.	安全,安全性 安全的;保密的
convenient	[kənˈviːniənt]	adj.	方便的;实用的
optional	[ˈɑːpʃənl]	adj.	可选择的,随意的
prevent	[prɪˈvent]	vt. vi.	预防,防止 妨碍,阻止
contribution	[ˌkɑːntrɪˈbjuːʃn]	n.	贡献;捐献
be requested to...			被要求做……

Part C Passage

1. Metro stations are divided into three categories according to the functions they serve

Simple stations, whose only mission is to serve the area surrounding the station transfer stations, serving transfers between lines of the same metro network interchanges, where there is connection with other transport modes (trams, buses, suburban rail services, etc.).

The stations constitute structural components of the system that are not usually constructed with the TBM(Tunnel Boring Machine). This is due to their usually rectangular cross section, their different dimensions with respect to the tunnels and, most importantly, due to their own different cross section transversally to the alignment.

The stations are usually constructed by excavation which requires the occupation of space on the ground surface, with all that this entails for the traffic in the city and for the activities of its inhabitants.

In this context, it is imperative that a complete study of the system's stations be performed before the beginning of the construction of the metro system. This is because, if certain construction and design options are not carefully and appropriately considered, there is an increased risk of failures and malfunctions either directly or in the mid-term; this will result in actual construction cost that is significantly higher than the initially estimated cost.

It should be noted that the construction of stations increases the total construction cost by 25%-30%, while the construction of an underground station is 4-6 times more expensive than the construction of a surface station.

Three of the main design/construction issues of a metro system that are of concern to the engineers during the phase of the project construction are:

The location/selection for stations;

The depth of their construction;

The method by which a station is constructed, as well as some of its structural elements.

The above three construction criteria are influenced by many parameters which influence one another, a fact that renders the selection a difficult task. The adoption of a suitable solution is a matter of knowledge, study and research; however, the experience gained from similar projects remains an irreplaceable asset for both designers and constructors.

2. Location selection for metro stations

The location of metro stations is studied in accordance with the servicing of network users and, generally, the servicing of areas where there is a high travel demand. The unsuitable selection of the locations of stations can lead to failures and malfunctions such as increased walking time for pedestrians, lack of service for locations that constitute transport generators, unsuitable service for areas with increased travel demand (universities, stadiums, hospitals, etc.) and inability to service "park-and-ride" facilities. Finally, some external factors arising from the location of the stations (such as the expropriation of areas where the stations will be built), if not properly

PART THREE FACILITIES PART 设施篇

addressed, they may result in delays in the stations' construction as well as in an increase in the construction cost.

The location selection for the metro stations depends on the trip characteristics of potential users: One of the issues that need be addressed initially is to determine the number of persons who want to travel, where they want to go, when and how often. To collect this information, appropriate transport studies are necessary. The selected location of the stations must serve the travel demand: In existing open spaces (public squares or small parks); On sidewalks, if the required space is available; In existing buildings.

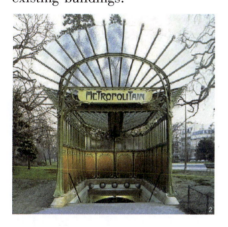

New Words and Expressions

interchange	[ˈɪntətʃeɪndʒ]	n.	（思想、信息等的）交换,互换,枢纽站
		v.	交换,互换
connection	[kəˈnekʃn]	n.	连接;关系;人脉;连接件
component	[kəmˈpoʊnənt]	n.	成分;组件,元件
		adj.	组成的;构成的

| alignment | [əˈlaɪnmənt] | n. | 队列,成直线;校准 |
| appropriately | [əˈproʊpriətli] | adv. | 适当地;合适地;相称地 |

1. How many kinds of metro stations according to the functions they serve?

2. What the location selection for the metro stations depends on?

Do you know any other metro stations? Please write them down.

1. metro station entrances   地铁站入口
2. merto station exit   地铁站出口
3. location selection for metro station   地铁站选址
4. metro station style   地铁车站风格

PART THREE   FACILITIES PART 设施篇

5. direct telephone inter-station   地铁站间行车电话
6. direct connection telephone inside station   地铁站内直通电话
7. construction depth of metro stations   地铁站施工深度
8. construction of the metro station's shell   地铁站顶施工

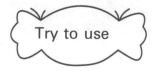

1. Talk about metro station in different cities.
_____.
2. What is the function of metro station?
_____.

Unit 14 Platforms 站台

Learning Objectives

After learning this unit, you should

* Understand some vocabularies about platform;
* Masterthe function of platform;
* Be able to introduce platform.

Advised Hours

4 class hours.

PART THREE　FACILITIES PART 设施篇

What are the functions of platform?

What are the platform facilities?

A: Would you please brief the platform facilities?

B: The specific facility is the must, for example elevators and lifts. Sometimes, the platform is the transit center of other public transportation then the bus transit signs metro transit signs will be displayed in nearest points. And commercial area including food court shops, studios, parking could occupy bigger area.

A: How can I deal with emergency broadcasting?

B: "Dear passengers, your attention please! Please leave the train along the nearest emergency exit directions, and assembly in platform. This metro needs a checkup urgently. We apologize for any inconvenience caused to you by the breakdown..." You will hear about it together with alarms no matter in which corner you are. Each platform has been facilitated for emergency as mentioned just now.

A: In this case, I'm wondering that the space of the platform is big enough to exercise emergency site order?

B: Definitely. The platform is designed according to feasibility data. Site space or equipments can meet the requirement of its populations.

A: Thank you. One more question, how should I deal with terminated service?

B: Sure, passengers will wonder it as well. As soon as we get site order under control, we will update them in the broadcasting, "Your attention please. Train service is suspended due to the emergency happened. We apologize for any inconvenience this might cause. The upcoming shifting train shall reach soon, or, the train has been terminated/cancelled, please transit to other public transports. Your comprehension and cooperation will be highly appreciated!"

A: Thanks a lot for your kindly explanation.

B: That's my pleasure!

commercial	[kə'mɜːrʃl]	n. adj.	商业广告 商业的;营利的;
emergency	[ɪ'mɜːrdʒənsi]	n. adj.	紧急情况;突发事件; 紧急的;备用的
broadcasting	['brɔːdkæstɪŋ]	n.	播放;广播节目
inconvenience	[ˌɪnkən'viːniəns]	vt. n.	麻烦;打扰 不便;麻烦
facilitate	[fə'sɪlɪteɪt]	V.	促进;帮助
comprehension	[ˌkɑːmprɪ'henʃn]	n.	理解;包含

Part C Passage

Platforms are the areas where boarding and alighting of passengers to and from the trains take place. At the same time, platforms also serve as waiting areas for the passengers.

1. Layout of platforms

The platforms can be placed either between the two main tracks (central platform), or at both sides of each track (side platforms), while side platforms can also be placed on entirely different levels within a station.

The layout of the central platform is the most economical solution; however, it often causes jams in passenger flows while requiring very careful marking to guide and orientate passengers.

In some stations, the central platform is accompanied by two side platforms. Although this solution requires more space, it is functionally ideal because it allows the boarding of passengers from the central platform and the alighting of passengers on the side ones.

2. Platform dimensions

The width of the platform is determined by the anticipated traffic during peak hours. The minimum width of the platform is 2.5 m while the usual width is between 3.5 and 4.0 m. Greater widths are foreseen for busy stations.

In the area of the platforms, no columns should be present as they obstruct passenger movements and reduce visibility.

Depending on the platform's use, its surface can be divided into the following zones:

The safety zone, with a width of 0.5 m measured from the edge of the platform which should not be used.

The concentration zone, which be used by passengers waiting to board the trains. The density of passengers in this zone is estimated at 2 persons/m².

The traffic zone, located behind the concentration zone, with a width of about 1.5 m for the movement of passengers alighting from the trains.

The equipment area is actually the remaining width of the platform. Cash desks, electronic ticketing distributors and so on are placed in this zone.

The total width of the platform depends to a large extent on the importance that is given to the concentration zone in relation to the variation in the number of passengers boarding the trains.

Regarding the height of the platform, it should be such that when the train is stopped, the vehicle's floor is on no occasion lower than the level of the platform's floor.

The gap between the floor of a stopped vehicle and the platform must be minimized. Usually this gap should be a few centimeters wide and no more than 5 cm.

New Words and Expressions

platform	[ˈplætfɔːrm]	n.	月台,站台,讲台
alight	[əˈlaɪt]	v. adj.	从(公共汽车、火车等)下来 闪亮的,神采飞扬的
orientate	[ˈɔːriənteɪt]	v.	朝向;确定方向;使熟悉
anticipated	[ænˈtɪsəˌpeɪtɪd]	adj.	预期的;期望的
zone	[zoʊn]	n.	地带;地区
dimension	[daɪˈmenʃn] [dɪˈmenʃn]	n. adj. vt.	方面;容积 规格的 标出尺寸

PART THREE　FACILITIES PART 设施篇

| density | [ˈdensəti] | n. | 密度 |

1. Why do some stations have two side platforms on the central platform?
_____.

2. Why the gap between the floor of a stopped vehicle and the platform, must be minimized?
_____.

Do you know any other platforms? Please write them down.
_____.

1. platform dimension　站台尺寸
2. the width of the platform　站台宽度
3. central platform　中央站台
4. layout of platform　站台布局

5. island platform 岛式站台

6. side platform 侧式站台

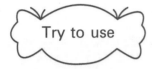

1. What is side platform?
   _____.

2. Which platform layout do you like?
   _____.

PART THREE   FACILITIES PART 设施篇

Unit 15 Metro Depot Facilities
地铁回车场设施

Learning Objectives

After learning this unit, you should
* Understand some vocabularies about metro depot facilities;
* Master metro depots;
* Be able to introduce metro depot facilities.

Advised Hours

4 class hours.

Do you know the facilities at the metro depot?

What are the functions of metro depot facilities?

A: Could you tell me where the subway park after work?

B: Sure. All will be at the metro depot, which is just nearby the station or terminals.

A: So could you introduce it?

B: Well, metro depot is located nearby station or in terminals. Where to park the metro depends on its operation plan or daily performance.

A: Whether all metro depots allowed to park?

B: Not really, metro lines are distinguished as fully operational and partly operational. Usually, metro listed in a roster is not allowed to park, because they shall implement the operation plan as scheduled on time.

A: How do we know which depot shall the metro park in?

B: It depends on their working number and their location in relation to the main line of the metro network. Each depot carries on specific missions. Some depots intake only parking, light maintenance or inspection. As if the metro requires full-scale maintenance, we will book a parking lot in exact depot

PART THREE FACILITIES PART 设施篇

which is well facilitated then.

A: It's like a patient to do registration of different departments in a hospital.

B: Correct! You've got the point.

 New Words and Expressions

terminal	[ˈtɜːrmɪnl]	n. adj.	终点站;终端机 末端的;终点的
depot	[ˈdiːpoʊ]	n. vt.	仓库;停车场 把…存放在储藏处
operational	[ˌɑːpəˈreɪʃənl]	adj.	操作的;运作的
implement	[ˈɪmplɪmɛnt]	vt. n.	实施,使生效 工具,手段
maintenance	[ˈmeɪntənəns]	n.	维护,保持;生活费用
inspection	[ɪnˈspekʃn]	n.	视察,检查
It depends on...			这取决于……

Part C Passage

Metro depots, depending on the activities performed, are distinguished as fully operational and partly operational.

In a metro network, as in the case of trams, the depot is of particular importance for the efficiency of the system.

The metro system is characterized by continuous extensions and dynamic adaptation to the passengers' transport requirements, resulting in changes in the fleet size and, consequently, changes in its maintenance requirements. Therefore, while during the construction of a new metro system, the construction of a fully operational depot constitutes common practice; this is not the case with the depots that are constructed at a later stage to serve the network expansions.

When there is more than one depot in a network, an allocation of the performed activities among the available depots is very often the selected option by the system operator.

Depending on their number and their location in relation to the main line of the network, some depots perform only specific activities (e. g. , only parking, light maintenance or inspection), while others offer full-scale maintenance facilities.

The first stage of the design of a new metro depot is the selection of the area where it will be built. The geographic position of the depot is selected based on the following criteria:

Sufficient ground plan area; acceptable length of dead vehicle kilometers; slight landscape (small height variations across its area); availability of suitable land; ability to integrate the depot into the existing land use — ability to access the road.

The planning and dimensioning process is difficult due to the great disparity between different metro systems and the lack of standards.

Metro depots exhibit major differences in comparison with tram depots. More specifically different horizontal alignment radii R_c are adopted. For tramway depots, a minimum horizontal alignment radius of R_c = 17-18 m is used, preferably R_c = 20 m, while for metro depots, a radius of R_c = 70-80 m is used.

The length of parking and maintenance tracks in the respective areas is different between the two depot types, since the metro trains are longer (60-150 m) than those of the tramway (30-45 m). However, it should be clarified that metro vehicles can be detached from the train and can be led individually to the maintenance tracks.

Inthe case of the metro, the depot is usually located close, yet outside the urban area, as opposed to the case of the tramway, where it is normally required to search for an area within or at the boundaries of the urban area.

The metro network usually has a radial shape. This allows for more options in searching for an area for the construction of the depot. The tramway network usually has a "linear" shape which reduces the options for the depot site considerably.

PART THREE   FACILITIES PART 设施篇

The two depots require different facilities for the maintenance of the bogies (due to the different floor heights of the vehicles). The larger size of the engineering equipment that is used at the metro depot and the higher number of electronic and other systems, in comparison with the tramway, result in a requirement for larger maintenance areas and more staff.

The comparatively large horizontal alignment radii that are adopted at metro depots render the construction of the ring track (loop line), which interconnects the various facilities, more difficult, compared to tramway depots. This fact mainly imposes the entry and exit to the parking and maintenance area from the same area (i.e. through bidirectional train movement). Also, having an access redundancy, that is, with two entry/exit points for the trains, is considered as a significant operational advantage.

As in the case of tramway systems, the estimate of the depot's ground plan area is an important tool in the selection process. Experts (2015) attempt an estimate of the required ground plan area of the premises and facilities of a metro depot with the aid of data collected from metro depots that are either existing or under construction.

More specifically, after statistical analyses, the average values of the surface area of the individual installations and of the total ground plan area of the depot per train of the design fleet were calculated.

New Words and Expressions

distinguished	[dɪˈstɪŋgwɪʃt]	adj. v.	卓越的,著名的 辨别;看清
extension	[ɪkˈstenʃn]	n.	拓展;延伸
dynamic	[daɪˈnæmɪk]	adj. n.	动态的;动力的 动态;动力
allocation	[ˌæləˈkeɪʃn]	n.	分配,配置;安置
geographic	[ˌdʒiəˈgræfɪk]	adj.	地理的;地理学的
comparison	[kəmˈpærɪsn]	n.	比较;对照;比较关系
detached	[dɪˈtætʃt]	v. adj.	拆卸;挣脱;派遣;可方便地取下 单独的
comparison with...			与……相比
detached from...			从……分离;拆卸

1. Why is the depot particularly important for the efficiency of the system?

2. Why is the tramway network usually in a "linear" shape?

PART THREE   FACILITIES PART 设施篇

Do you know the reason why the two depots require different facilities for the maintenance of the bogies? Please write it down.

1. metro depot   地铁停车场
2. transit depot   中转站
3. depot's ground   停车场地面
4. fixed signal/wayside signal   地面信号
5. metro network   地铁线网
6. crossing signal   道口信号

1. What are the functions of metro depots?

2. What is the transit depot?

PART FOUR VEHICLE PART
车 辆 篇

Unit 16 Electric Locomotive 电力机车

Learning Objectives

After learning this unit, you should

* Understand some vocabularies about electric locomotive;
* Master types of electric locomotive;
* Be able to introduce the electric locomotive.

Advised Hours

4 class hours.

PART FOUR VEHICLE PART 车辆篇

locomotive operators

Are the locomotive operators all male?

A: Does every locomotive have an operator?

B: Yes. Every locomotive has a full-time operator, it's equipped from beginning.

A: Does China have a time table for unmanned technology of metro system?

B: That's the latest tech. at present. It does work in some countries. But China is still researching it. It's hot topic to fans in different field. Just like we expect driverless taxi appear in China also.

A: Are the operators all male?

B: Train operation is manual work. Look at the aviation, how many ladies working as pilot? Same in locomotive, we've experienced operator ladies here. They can operate it as good as a man.

A: Then, how to operate the locomotive?

B: It's almost an automatic system actually. A operator needs to keep an eye on those buttons and console, handle it in time as system requested. In case operator operation failed, our monitoring center will take measures immediately to keep all under control. That's the backup security proposal.

New Words and Expressions

unmanned	[ˌʌnˈmænd]	adj.	无人的；无人操纵的
aviation	[ˌeɪviˈeɪʃn]	n.	航空；飞行术；飞机制造业
pilot	[ˈpaɪlət]	n. adj.	飞行员；领航员 试点的
console	[kənˈsəʊl]	n. vt.	[电] 操纵台；支撑架 安慰；慰藉
monitoring	[ˈmɒnɪtərɪŋ]	n.	监视，[自] 监控；检验，检查
keep an eye on...			密切注视……

Part C Passage

An electric locomotive is a non-autonomous locomotive, which receives electrical power for its motion from an external electrical supply source.

The general scheme for the electrical power supply system used on electrified railways is presented in the following figure. The electricity from the power plant is transmitted to traction substations over the high-voltage distribution power lines. The substations perform the transformation of the current in accordance with the parameters required and then supply it through feeder power lines to points along the overhead

PART FOUR　　VEHICLE PART　车辆篇

line equipment for powering electric locomotives through the contact conductor wire. For closed-loop networks, the railway track is equipped with special return feeders which are connected to the power substations.

1-power station; 2-distribution power lines; 3-electrical traction substation; 4-feeder power line; 5-overhead line equipment; 6-return feeder

Electric locomotives can be divided into three types: Direct current (DC) electric locomotives; Alternating current (AC) electric locomotives; Multi-system electric locomotives. Electric locomotives can be designed to operate on either DC or AC, or selectively operate on both. Furthermore, the voltage of DC and AC as well as the frequencies of ACs can be different on different railways.

The following figure shows one of the equipment layout options for an AC electric locomotive. DC electric locomotives are different from AC ones because they do not have high-voltage AC electrical power, therefore they do not have a step-down transformer for feeding the DC traction motors.

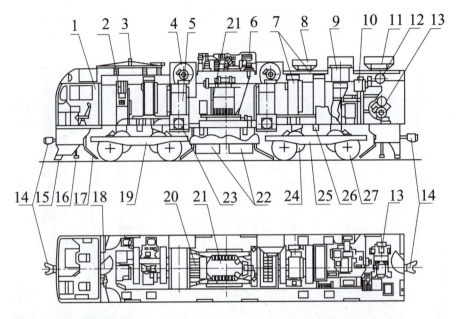

1-driver cab; 2-cabinet with electrical equipment and microprocessor control system; 3-pantograph; 4-front bogie cooling fan system; 5-inverter; 6-high-voltage input equipment; 7-cabinet with electrical equipment; 8-main transformer oil cooling system reservoir; 9-set of brake resistors; 10-propulsion rectifier; 11-brake pneumatic system main reservoir; 12-brake pneumatic system auxiliary reservoir; 13-air compressor; 14-coupler; 15-headstock; 16-locomotive signaling system coil receiver; 17-sand trap; 18-parking brake; 19-front bogie; 20-capacitor block; 21-main transformer unit; 22-batteries; 23-smoothing reactors; 24-traction motor; 25-rear bogie; 26-pivot; 27-wheelset

Multi-system electric locomotives have the current collection, traction and power equipment required for working with several different combinations of current and voltage. An electric locomotive consists of the following basic systems: electrical, mechanical, pneumatic and hydraulic.

The car body, main frame, coupling devices, suspension, devices for transmission of tractive and brake efforts, bogies and asystem for air cooling and ventilation of the electric traction equipment belong to the mechanical system of an electric locomotive.

The pneumatic system includes an air compressor which supplies compressed air through connecting pipelines to the brake system as well as an automatic control system, reservoirs for storage of the compressed air, and control and management systems and instrumentation (valves, manometers, etc.).

Contact conductor, power transformers, inverters, traction electric motors, auxiliary machines, electrical control and management units, and the dynamic and regenerative braking systems are all parts of the electrical equipment of electric locomotives.

The hydraulic system includes liquid cooling systems (oil, water, etc.) of electric locomotives, and also a hydraulic control system and instrumentation.

On electric locomotives, the following types of traction motors can be used:
- Brushed DC electric motors;
- AC motors;
- Brushless DC electric motors.

Traction motors are used in the current designs for the dynamic and regenerative brakes with the purpose of reducing wear of the contact parts of the mechanical and hydraulic brake systems, and also for economy of electrical power consumption.

During dynamic braking, the electric energy dissipates as heat from variable resistors; but, in the case of regenerative braking, this energy is fed back into the electrical power contact network, or into on-board storage in the case of hybrid locomotives.

Brushless DC electric and AC motors are the most promising because they produce a large tractive effort and they have smaller dimensions and weight in comparison with brushed DC motors as well as reduced costs for operation, maintenance and repair processes.

New Words and Expressions

autonomous	[ɔːˈtɑːnəməs]	adj.	自治的;自主的;自发的
non-autonomous			非自主
distribution	[ˌdɪstrɪˈbjuːʃn]	n.	分布;分配;供应

feeder	[ˈfiːdər]	n.	支线;饲养员;支流
suspension	[səˈspenʃn]	n.	悬浮;悬架;暂停;停职
regenerative	[rɪˈdʒenərətɪv]	adj.	再生的,更生的;更新的
dissipate	[ˈdɪsɪpeɪt]	vt. vi.	浪费;使……消散 驱散;放荡
be used in...			用于……
consists of...			由……组成……

Try to understand

1. What are the types of electric locomotives?

2. What is the difference between direct current and alternating current?

Part D Word Power

Try to collect

Do you know the electric locomotive components? Please write them down.

PART FOUR　VEHICLE PART 车辆篇

Part E Language Use

Try to read

1. electric locomotive　电力机车
2. vehicle body　车体
3. locomotive signaling system coil receiver　电力机车信号系统线圈接收器
4. parking brake　驻车制动器
5. cabinet with electrical equipment　电器柜
6. brushed DC electric motors　有刷直流电动机

Try to use

1. What is locomotive signaling system coil receiver?

2. What is parking brake?

Unit 17 Bogies 转向架

Learning Objectives

After learning this unit, you should

* Understand some vocabularies about bogies;
* Master bogies with frame-mounted traction motors;
* Be able to introduce bogies.

Advised Hours

4 class hours.

PART FOUR VEHICLE PART 车辆篇

Part A Lead-in

Do you know what is bogies?

What is the function of bogies?

Part B Dialogue

A: Would you tell me the classification of China Subway?

B: Well, most of trains are 6-carriage unit. But in Beijing and Shanghai, the most popular lines are equipped with 10-carriage, which still can't meet the demands of rush hours.

A: Are they motor cars?

B: Each car is a motor car.

A: How to control the limited loading in each carriage and ensure the door system work as usual?

B: Doors are controlled by the TO in the cab. Most of time, we've no problems with daily loading. Passengers are mostly well educated and obey public rules. Unfortunately, in public holidays and rush hours, it's almost out of control. That's why we will pay more attention on safety at the moment.

A: That'll be stressful.

B: Yeah, the working time will be longer than usual.

New Words and Expressions

classification	[ˌklæsɪfɪˈkeɪʃn]	n.	分类;类别;等级
carriage	[ˈkærɪdʒ]	n.	运输;运费;举止;客车厢
demand	[dɪˈmænd]	n. / v.	需求 / 强烈要求;查问,查询
equip	[ɪˈkwɪp]	vt.	装备,配备
rush hours			上下班高峰时间

Part C Passage

Locomotive Traction Drives

Traction drives are made up of mechanisms and units engaged in the transfer of kinematic power from the traction motors (electric, hydraulic) or the output shaft of the mechanical gear transmission to the wheelsets or wheels of the powered rail vehicle. Designs of drives are varied and depend on the types and operational service parameters of rail traction vehicles, the selected mode of transmission, the design of wheelsets/wheels and the mounting methods of the traction motor. The traction drive designs can be divided into two types: individual or grouped.

For the individual drive design, the traction torque from the motor acts on one wheelset or one wheel. An example of such a design is shown in the following figure. For the grouped drive design, the traction torque from the motor or an output shaft of transmission is shared between multiple wheelsets or bogie wheels. The mono motor bogie has a grouped drive design.

The design and parameters of traction drives are often dependent on the installation designs of traction motors and associated gearing. Three design variants have found wide application:

With a nose-suspended traction motor;
With a frame-mounted traction motor;
With a body-mounted traction motor.

Generally, the first of these design variants has traction drives, of which one part is resting on the axle of the wheelset through rolling or slip bearings, and the other part is connected through the elastic-damping suspension to the frame of a bogie or the locomotive. Torque from the motor is transmitted to the gear box, the driven gear of which is seated firmly on the axle. The advantage of this drive design is a low price and simplicity of design. It enables the effective transfer of high tractive effort. However, in this case about 60% of the weight of the engine and the traction gear account for unspring mass; this causes increased dynamic effects of the traction vehicle on the track. This type of suspension is widely used in locomotives with a relatively low design speed, usually on freight and shunting locomotives.

This design also has some potential modifications whereby the traction motor rests on and transmits traction torque to the wheelset via elastic elements. The modified design is a bit more complicated, but it leads to a significant reduction of dynamic impact loads which allow its use at higher speeds of up to 200 km/h.

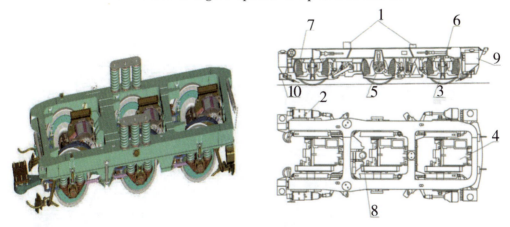

1-side bearing; 2-brake cylinder; 3-wheel set; 4-traction motor; 5-axle box; 6-damper; 7-coil spring; 8-yoke for the center pin; 9-sand box; 10-sand trap

The other two design variants are similar because the traction motor is mounted to the bogie frame or the main frame (car body). An example of a traction drive design with a body-mounted traction motor is shown in the following figure.

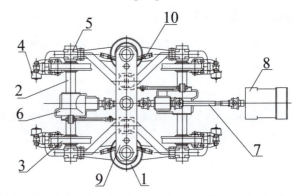

1-air spring; 2-axle; 3-wheel; 4-brake cylinder; 5-axle box; 6-gear box; 7-shaft; 8-body-mounted traction motor; 9-bolster; 10-damper

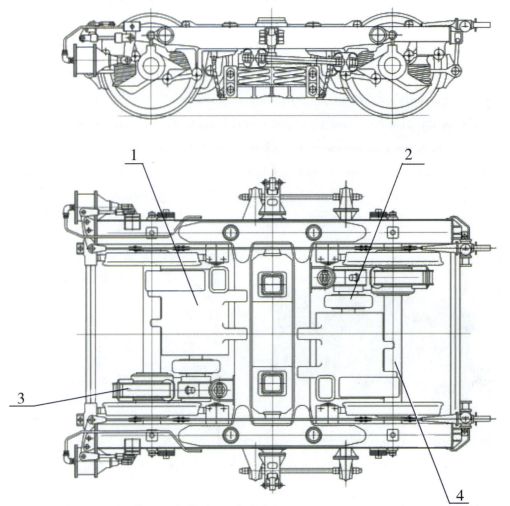

1-traction motor; 2-flexible coupling; 3-gear box; 4-wheelset

PART FOUR　VEHICLE PART 车辆篇

Another example with a frame-mounted traction motor is shown in the following figure.

New Words and Expressions

mechanism	[ˈmekənɪzəm]	n.	机制;原理;机械装置
kinematic	[ˌkɪnəˈmætɪk]	adj.	[力] 运动学上的,[力] 运动学的
parameter	[pəˈræmɪtər]	n.	参数;系数;参量
mounting	[ˈmaʊntɪŋ]	adj. n. v.	增加的 支座,装备 安排,镶嵌,安置
individual	[ˌɪndɪˈvɪdʒuəl]	adj. n.	个人的;个别的 个人,个体
installation	[ˌɪnstəˈleɪʃn]	n.	安装,装置;就职
axle	[ˈæksl]	n.	车轴;[车辆] 轮轴
variant	[ˈveriənt]	n. adj.	变体;转化 不同的;多样的
be engaged in...			从事于;忙于
elastic-damping			弹塑性阻尼

1. Which three design variants have found wide application?

2. What do the design and parameters of the traction drive often depend on?

Do you know other bogies? Please write them down.

_____
_____

1. bogie　转向架
2. bogie frame　转向构架
3. traction vehicle　牵引车辆
4. bogie wheels　轮对
5. shunting locomotive　调车电力机车
6. power supply mode　供电方式

1. What is the shunting locomotive?

_____

2. What is the traction vehicle?

_____

PART FOUR　VEHICLE PART 车辆篇

Unit 18　Pantographs
受电弓

Learning Objectives

After learning this unit, you should

* Understand some vocabularies about pantographs;

* Master the function of the pantographs;

* Be able to introduce the pantographs.

Advised Hours

4 class hours.

How many components does power supply system composited of in the subway?

Why does the signal system have two power supplies?

A: How many components does power supply system composited of in the subway?

B: Generally, we have city electricity.

A: Why does the signal system have two power supplies?

B: One of the supplies is common daily supply, another is the backup of safety of its normal work. The signal system is lifeline of subway operation. We can't imagine how it would be, if power cut off. Besides loss in the economics, no one can accept casualties. It's many families' happiness concerned.

A: LV distributor got two power supplies, is it the same reason?

B: That's right. In metro system, most working system got backup proposal, as if it's available, just in cases any emergency.

A: That's appreciated by all passengers.

 New Words and Expressions

| casualty | [ˈkæʒuəlti] | n. | 伤员,亡者 |

Part C Passage

A pantograph is a device that collects electric current from overhead lines for electric trains or trams. The term stems from the resemblance to pantograph devices for copying writing and drawings.

Early (1895) flat pantograph on a Baltimore & Ohio Railroad electric locomotive. The contact ran inside the section bar, so both lateral and vertical flexibility was necessary. A flat side-pantograph was invented in 1895 at the Baltimore & Ohio Railroad and in Germany in 1900 by Siemens. The familiar diamond-shaped roller pantograph was invented by John Q. Brown of the Key System shops for their commuter trains which ran between San Francisco and the East Bay section of the San Francisco Bay Area in California. They appear in photographs of the first day of service at 26 October 1903. For many decades thereafter, the same diamond shape was used by electric rail systems around the world and remains in use by some today.

The pantograph was an improvement on the simple trolley pole which prevailed up to that time primarily because it allowed an electric rail vehicle to travel at higher speeds without losing contact with the catenary.

Electrical circuits require two connections (or for three phase AC, three connections). From the very beginning, the track work itself was used for one side of the circuit. Unlike model railroads, however, the track work normally supplies only one side, the other side(s) of the circuit being provided separately.

The original Baltimore and Ohio Railroad electrification used a sliding shoe in an overhead channel a system quickly found to be unsatisfactory. It was replaced with a third-rail system, in which a pickup (the "shoe") rode underneath or on top of a smaller rail parallel to the main track, somewhat above ground level. There were multiple pickups on both sides of the locomotive in order to accommodate the breaks in the third-rail required by track work. This system is preferred in subways because of the close clearances it affords.

However, railways generally tend to prefer overhead lines, often called "catenaries" after the support system used to hold the wire parallel to the ground. Three collection methods are possible:

Trolley pole: a long flexible pole, which engages the line with a wheel or shoe;

Bow collector: a frame that holds a long collecting rod against the wire;

Pantograph: a hinged frame that holds the collecting shoes against the wire in a fixed geometry.

Of the three, the pantograph method is best suited for high-speed operation. Some locomotives are equipped to use both overhead and third-rail collection (e. g. British Rail Class 92).

Pantographs easily adapt to various heights of the overhead wires by partly folding. The electric transmission system for modern electric rail systems consists of an upper weight carrying wire (known as a catenary) from which is suspended a contact wire. The pantograph is spring loaded and pushes a contact shoe up against the contact wire to draw the electricity needed to run the train. The steel rails on the tracks act as the electrical return. As the train moves, the contact shoe slides along the wire and can set up acoustical standing waves in the wires which break the contact and degrade current collection. This means that on some systems adjacent pantographs are not permitted.

New Words and Expressions

| pantograph | [ˈpæntəɡræf] | n. | 放大尺;受电弓 |

PART FOUR VEHICLE PART 车辆篇

resemblance	[rɪˈzembləns]	n.	相似;相似之处;相似物
catenary	[kəˈtinəri]	n.	接触网 链;悬链线;链状物
accommodate	[əˈkɑːmədeɪt]	vt. vi.	容纳;供应 适应;调解
replaced with...			替换为……
trolley pole			集电杆
set up			建立;装配;开业

1. How do electric trains or trams collect electric current from overhead lines?

2. What is the function of the pantograph?

Why do electrical circuits require two connections?

Part E Language Use

1. pantograph   受电弓
2. current collector   受流器
3. traction power supply system   牵引供电系统
4. electric rail vehicle   电动轨道车

1. How many kind of pantographs?

2. What is the function of the pantograph?

PART FOUR　VEHICLE PART 车辆篇

Unit 19　Pneumatic Brakes
气压制动

Learning Objectives

After learning this unit, you should

* Understand vocabularies about pneumatic brakes;
* Master train pneumatic brake model;
* Be able to introduce the pneumatic brakes.

Advised Hours

4 class hours.

Which kind of brake is equipped in metro?

How does pneumatic brake achieve its function?

A: Which kind of brake is equipped in metro?

B: It is pneumatic brake.

A: Do you know its basic components?

B: Basically, it has four parts.

A: Then how does pneumatic brake achieve its function?

B: It's quite complicated but with excellent performance. If I explain to you, mostly are technical words. I'm afraid you won't be interested.

A: oh, it sounds very difficult. Is it widely used? Any features?

B: Right, it's most popular in the field. It's a more practical and high-efficiency control system of whole vehicle.

 New Words and Expressions

| pneumatic | [nuːˈmætɪk] | adj. n. | 气动的；充气的 气胎 |

PART FOUR VEHICLE PART 车辆篇

complicate	[ˈkɑːmplɪkeɪt]	vt.	使复杂化；使恶化；使卷入
excellent	[ˈeksələnt]	adj.	卓越的；极好的；杰出的
performance	[pərˈfɔːrməns]	n.	性能；绩效；执行；表现
it sounds...			听起来……
high-efficiency		adj. n.	高效的 高效

Part C Passage

Pneumatic brakes or "air brakes" operate by use of a long "brake pipe" that runs down the length of the train. The brake pipe supplies air to a reservoir on each rail vehicle (except in some designs where the braking systems on permanently coupled wagons share reservoirs), and the pressure in the pipe acts as a signal to apply and release the brakes. The brake model is made up of two integrated pneumatic systems, one for the brake pipe and the other for the brake valve and reservoir on each rail vehicle. Fluid modeling techniques can be used to model the operation of these two combined systems.

Alternatively, empirical lookup tables are sometimes used to reduce the computational power required for train simulations. An empirical lookup table is typically created from experimental brake tests and is only valid for that particular train configuration, although models are sometimes modified for use with different train lengths. Empirical models are also only valid for the brake application amplitudes that have been measured. With railway brakes there are three main levels of brake application, these being minimum, full service and emergency. Various other "service" brake levels can range in magnitude from the "minimum" application to the "full service" application. An appropriate number of brake tests should be done to cover a suitable number of applications.

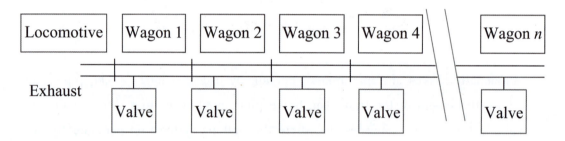

Empirical models may not accurately model the brakes when changes are made to the level of braking throughout the application. This may occur when an initial brake application is made and then the brake application level is subsequently increased or reduced. Empirical models are best used for modeling where only set brake applications are made with no changes in the braking level during the brake application.

Pneumatic rail vehicle brake systems can be quite intricate, with many reservoirs and valves. An example of a brake system that is used on heavy haul wagons is shown in the following figure.

Inside the triple valve there are more valves, chambers and chokes. While the air brake valve arrangement started its development as a simple system, more features have been continually added throughout its design lifetime to improve its performance. The general operation of the system is where the brake pipe is normally at a set pressure which charges the rail vehicle reservoirs, and a reduction in brake pipe pressure triggers the valve to actuate the brake cylinders. As the brake pipe is returned back to its maximum pressure, the rail vehicle brakes release.

PART FOUR   VEHICLE PART 车辆篇

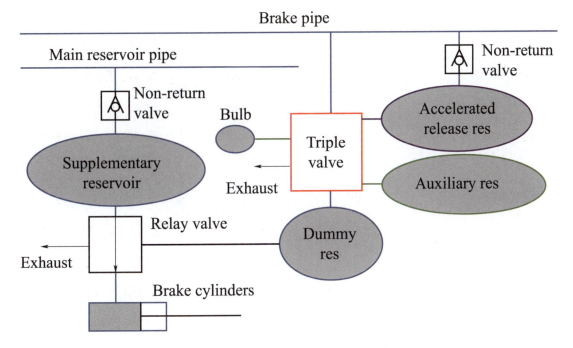

The brake valve can be modeled as a fluid system with the various valves and reservoirs. However, for the study of train dynamics, a mixture of fluid modeling and empirical modeling may be adequate to provide an accurate value for the final braking force. The internal operation of the brake valve is of little or no interest in the study of train dynamics. If an empirical model for the brake system is used, it is possible to include the entire system in the empirical model and thus eliminate the need to model each rail vehicle brake system individually. Fluid models of the brake pipe and rail vehicle brake systems are useful when studying how the brake system performance is affected by any changes to the brake system. What is not shown in the rail vehicle brake schematic is the load switch which causes a smaller braking force to be applied to empty or lighter rail vehicles. This is done to eliminate the possibility of wheel slip during braking. As the load switch is a simple on/off switch or a variable switch, this is relatively simple to model using the logic functions.

New Words and Expressions

| reservoir | [ˈrezərvwɑːr] | n. | 水库;蓄水池 |

integrated	[ˈɪntɪɡreɪtɪd]	adj. v.	综合的;完整的 整合;使…成整体
alternatively	[ɔːlˈtɜːrnətɪvli]	adv.	要不,或者
empirical	[ɪmˈpɪrɪkl]	adj.	经验主义的,完全根据经验的;实证的
computational	[ˌkɑːmpjuˈteɪʃnl]	adj.	计算的
cylinder	[ˈsɪlɪndər]	n.	圆筒;汽缸;圆柱状物
eliminate	[ɪˈlɪmɪneɪt]	vt.	消除;排除
made up			编造;做成的

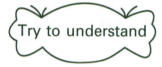

Try to understand

1. What does the brake model consist of?

2. What is the relay valve?

Part D Word Power

Try to collect

How is the pneumatic system composed? Please write it down.

PART FOUR VEHICLE PART 车辆篇

Part E Language Use

Try to read

1. emergency brake   紧急制动
2. emergency stop plunger   紧急制动按钮
3. electro pneumatic brake   电空制动
4. rail vehicle brake systems   轨道车辆制动系统
5. brake pipe   制动管
6. pneumatic brakes   气压制动器

Try to use

1. What is electro pneumatic brake?

2. What is the function of emergency stop plunger?

Unit 20 Maintenance and Management
维护与管理

Learning Objectives

After learning this unit, you should
* Understand some vocabularies about maintenance and management;
* Master track maintenance technologies;
* Be able to introduce maintenance and management.

Advised Hours

4 class hours.

PART FOUR   VEHICLE PART 车辆篇

What do you know about maintenance and management?

What factors may cause metro operation malfunction?

A: What factors may cause metro operation malfunction?

B: That could be a list of… capacity, vehicle, signal, track, power supply, etc.

A: What do you mean by capacity?

B: Capacity means the maximum loading. Same as other vehicles or transportations, limited quantity is always declared. That's the safe loading. As soon as the loading exceed the capacity during the rush hour, definitely, it will cause breakdown. And passengers may get hurt.

A: Oh, then how can it be improved, in case of that?

B: Platform Screen Doors are installed, which is synchronized with metro door opening and closing. Meanwhile, minimum one staff will stand by as signalman to do supervise it, including to evacuate passengers.

A: Anymore?

B: The alarm system also facilitated to warn passengers from time to time.

A: We need not only improve our technology, but also passenger's safety consciousness.

B: Right. That's the key point.

A: So it is very important to keep safe transports.

B: Absolutely.

New Words and Expressions

definitely	[ˈdefɪnətli]	adv.	清楚地,当然;明确地,肯定地
consciousness	[ˈkɑːnʃəsnəs]	n.	意识;知觉;觉悟
synchronized	[ˈsɪŋkrənaɪzd]	adj.	同步的;同步化的
synchronized with...			与……同步

Part C Passage

Track maintenance technologies are an integral part of a high-speed railway technology system. A set of scientific management system must be established, and the track equipment must be inspected, maintained, and repaired regularly and periodically for high performance in riding safety, quality, and comfort and for the serviceability of track equipment. In this regard, the principal role of track maintenance is to keep the track equipment in good status, allowing high-speed trains to travel safely, stably, comfortably, and uninterruptedly at specified speeds, as well as to prolong the service life of the equipment.

In China, prevention is the first concern in maintaining high-speed railways (HSRs), supplemented by control measures, strict inspection, and cautious maintenance processes. Specifically, maintenance work should be performed in an organized way, including accurate inspection, comprehensive analysis, and precise maintenance, as per the regularity of track status, to prevent and control possible track problems effectively. As a supplement, other maintenance management systems, such as inspection overhaul separation, specialized and district management of track equipment, maintenance skylight, information management of maintenance, and track maintenance based on a precise survey control network, are also applied.

The above maintenance principles and management systems are also applicable to high-speed turnouts. However, owing to the special features and important role in the safety of railway traffic as compared with common railway sections, the maintenance technologies for high-speed turnouts are somewhat different.

New Words and Expressions

integral	[ˈɪntɪɡrəl]	adj. / n.	完整的,整体的;构成整体所必需的部分;完整
scientific	[ˌsaɪənˈtɪfɪk]	adj.	科学的,系统的
periodically	[ˌpɪriˈɑːdɪkli]	adv.	定期地;周期性地
uninterruptedly	[ˈʌnɪntəˈrʌptɪdli]	adv.	不间断地;连续地
prevention	[prɪˈvenʃn]	n.	预防;阻止;妨碍
supplement	[ˈsʌpləˌmɛnt]	v.	增补,补充
principle	[ˈprɪnsəpl]	n.	原则;本质;根源

1. What are track maintenance technologies?

2. What is the first concern in maintaining high-speed railways, in China?

Do you know what things involve in maintenance work? Please write them down.

_____.

1. metro operation malfunction   地铁运行故障
2. alarm systems   报警系统
3. common railway sections   常见铁路部分
4. track maintenance technologies   跟踪维护技术
5. high-speed railways   高速铁路
6. maintenance management system   维修管理系统

1. What is metro operation malfunction?

_____.

2. What is alarm systems?

_____.

附录 Appendix

附录1：地下铁道列车车票使用办法

第一条 为加强本市地下铁道列车车票的使用管理，维护乘车秩序，根据国家和本市有关规定，制定本办法。

第二条 乘坐地下铁道列车的乘客（以下简称乘客），须照章购票，接受验票，凭票乘车。禁止不购票或用废票、假票乘车。

（一）普通单张票，在购票站当日乘车有效。

（二）乘客带领一个身高不满1.2米的儿童乘车，儿童免票；带领两个以上身高不满1.2米的儿童乘车，一个儿童免票。

（三）持有免费乘车证的伤残军人、盲人，可免费乘车。免费乘车证只限持证者本人使用，但一名盲人可有一名陪同人员免票。

（四）乘客使用各站通用的本票乘车时，须由站务员验票和撕票。乘客自行从本票上撕下的车票，视为废票。

（五）已使用过的车票为废票，不得再次使用。车票售出，不予退票。

第三条 使用月票的乘客，须遵守下列规定：

（一）月票限当月按照规定的次数使用。

（二）购有月票但未随身携带的，乘车时应照章购票。

（三）禁止使用过期的月票乘车，禁止冒用、涂改或伪造月票。

第四条 不按规定购票、用票的乘客，须按下列规定补交票款：

（一）使用过期月票的，自票面标明月份次月第一日起至发现日止，每日按普通单张票票价4倍的金额补交票款，但补交票款的总额不超过300元。

（二）冒用、涂改、伪造月票的，没收其月票，并补交票款100元。

（三）使用假票、废票的，或不接受验票，无票通过验票口的，按普通单张票票价的10倍金额补交票款。

乘客补交票款后，由站务员出具补票凭证。

第五条　乘客不按规定购票、用票，且拒绝补票或验票，扰乱公共交通秩序的，移送公安机关依法处理。

第六条　本办法经人民政府批准，自发布之日起施行。

Regulations on Subway Maps Tickets

Article 1

These regulations are formulated in accordance with national and municipal regulations to ensure the proper use of subway tickets.

Article 2

Passengers shall purchase tickets to ride on the subway. Those without tickets or those who use invalid or counterfeit tickets may not board the subway.

（1）Single tickets are only valid on the date of issue.

（2）One passenger may take one child below 1.2 m free of charge; should two or more such children be taken, only one child may enjoy a free trip.

（3）Disabled servicemen and blind persons who hold a Free Boarding Card may take the subway free of charge. The card is valid only for the cardholder, but an accompanying person may take a free trip.

（4）Passengers with a General Ticket-pad shall have the ticket checked and torn off at the ticket check. Any torn-off by the passenger himself/herself will render the ticket void.

（5）Expired ticket will be considered null and void. Tickets are not refundable once sold.

Article 3

Passengers using monthly tickets shall abide by the following rules：

（1）The monthly ticket shall only be valid within the month. Its use shall be frequency-limited.

（2）A regular ticket shall be purchased by holders of a monthly ticket if the monthly ticket is not carried on the holder.

（3）No expired, altered or counterfeit monthly ticket shall be used.

Article 4

Passengers that fail to purchase or use tickets as required shall be liable to the following surcharges：

（1）Users of an expired ticket shall pay four times the daily charge for an ordinary single ticket for each day counted from the first day of the month as indicated on the monthly ticket until the day when the offence is discovered. No surcharge, however, shall exceed 300 yuan.

（2）Users of an altered or counterfeit monthly ticket shall have the ticket confiscated and pay a surcharge of 100 yuan.

（3）Persons who use a counterfeit or expired ticket, or enter the station without a ticket, shall pay a surcharge 10 times of a single ticket.

Article 5

Passengers who fail to purchase or use tickets as required and refuse to undergo ticket inspection or pay surcharges shall be handed over to the police if the case is serious enough to disrupt public order.

Article 6

These regulations have been approved by the People's Government Municipality and shall enter into force when promulgated.

附录2：英文数字、算式表示法

一、小数表示法

1. 小数用基数词来表示,以小数点为界,小数点左侧的数字表示整数,数字合起来读;小数点右侧的数字表示小数,数字分开来读;小数点读作 point,0 读作 zero 或 o[ou],整数部分为零时,可以省略不读。例如:0.4 读作 zero point four 或 point four;10.23 读作 ten point two three;25.67 读作 twenty-five point six seven;1.03 读作 one point o three。

2. 当数字值大于1时,小数后面的名词用复数,数字值小于1时,小数后面的名词用单数。例如:1.03 meters,0.49 ton,1.5 tons。

二、分数表示法

分数是由基数词和序数词一起来表示的。基数词作分子,序数词作分母,除了分子是"1"以外,其他情况下序数词都要用复数形式。例如:3/4 读作 three fourths,或读作 three quarters;1/3 读作 one third,或读作 a third;24/25 读作 twenty-four twenty-fifths;3 又 1/4 读作 three and one fourth,或读作 three and one quarter;1/2 读作 a half;1/4 读作 one quarter,或读作 a quarter;1 又 1/2 读作 one and a half;1 又 1/4 读作 one and a quarter。当分数后面接名词时,如果分数表示的值大于1,名词用复数;小于1,名词用单数。例如:1 又 1/2 hours 读作 one and a half hours;2 又 3/4 meters 读作 two and three-fourths meters。

三、百分数表示法

百分数用基数 + percent 表示。例如:50% 读作 fifty percent;3% 读作 three percent;0.12 % 读作 zero point one two percent。这里的 percent 前半部 per 表示"每",后半部分 cent 表示 "百",所以百分之几中 percent 不用复数形式。

四、加、减、乘、除和乘方表示法

1. "加"用 plus、and 或 add 表示;"等于"用 is、make、equal 等词表示。例如:2 + 3 = ? 可表示为:How much is wo plus three? ;2 + 3 = 5 有如下几种表示:Two plus three is five. Two and three is equal to five. Two and three make five. Two added to three equals five. If we add two to/and three, we get five.

2. "减"用 minus 或 take from 表示。例如:10 - 6 = ? 有如下几种表示:How much is ten minus six? 10 - 6 = 4 ten minus six is four. Take six from ten and the remainder is four. Six (taken) from ten is four.

3. "乘"用 time (动词) 或 multiply 表示。例如:3 × 4 = ? 有如下几种表示:How much is three times four? 3 × 4 = 12 Three times four is/are twelve. Multiply three by four, we get twelve. Three multiplied by four makes twelve.

4. "除"用 divide 的过去分词形式表示。例如:16 ÷ 4 = ? 有如下几种表示:How much is sixteen divided by four? 16 ÷ 4 = 4 sixteen divided by four is four. Sixteen divided by four equals/gives/makes four.

五、数量表示法

表示长、宽、高、面积等,用基数词 + 单位词 (meter、foot、inch、kilogram 等) + 形容词 (long、wide、high 等) 表示,或者用基数词 + 单位词 + in + 名词 (length、width、height、weight 等) 表示。例如:two meters long 或 two meters in length 2;three feet high 或 three feet in height 3;four inches wide 或 four inches in width;This box is 2 kilograms in weight. The city wall of Xi'an is 12 meters wide and 12 meters high.

附录3:公共信息中英文对照

警示提示信息

1. 暂停服务　Temporarily Out of Service

2. 暂停收款　Temporarily Closed

3. 顾客止步　Staff Only

4. 禁止通过　No Admittance

5. 营业时间　Open Hours/ Business Hours

6. 请扶好站好　Please Use Handrail

7. 票款当面点清/找零请当面点清　Please Check Your Change Before Leaving

8. 进入超市请先存包　Please Deposit Your Bags

9. 请勿将饮料带入场内　No Drinks from Outside

10. 请排队等候入场　Please Line Up

11. 请保持场内清洁　Please Keep the Area Clean/Don't Litter

12. 请关闭通信设备　Please Turn Off Cellphones & Beepers

13. 请将手机和寻呼机静音　Please Mute Cellphones & Beepers

14. 禁止未成年人进入　Adults Only

企业名称及业态类信息

1. ××大厦　×× Tower/Plaza/Mansion/ Building

2. 贸易中心　Trade Center

3. 商场　Store

4. 百货商场　Department Store

5. 购物中心　Shopping Center

6. 大型购物中心　Shopping Mall

7. 超市　Supermarket

8. 便利店　Convenience Store

9. 汽车4S店　4S Auto Shop

10. 食品店　Food Store

11. 电器城　Home Appliances Store /Home Appliances Center

12. 出租车区域　Taxi Area

13. 眼镜店　Optical Shop

14. 药店　Pharmacy

15. 书店　Bookstore

16. 酒吧　Bar/Pub

17. 形象设计中心　Image Design Center

18. 发型工作室　Hair Studio

19. 餐馆　Restaurant

20. 美食城　Food Palace

21. 美食街　Food Street/ Food Court

22. 美食广场　Food Plaza

23. 中式快餐　Chinese Fast Food

24. 共享充电宝　Sharable Chargers

25. 无线网络服务区　Wireless Network Service Area

26. 吸烟区　Smoking Service Area

27. 母婴室　Mother and Baby Room

28. 共享单车　Bike-sharing Area

其他

1. 座　Seat
2. 排　Row
3. 东区　East Area
4. 南区　South Area
5. 西区　West Area
6. 北区　North Area
7. 单号　Odd Numbers
8. 双号　Even Numbers
9. 贵宾区　VIP Area
10. 公众区　Public Area
11. 办公区　Administrative Area
12. 看台区　Audience Area

附录4：常用缩略语

一、地铁管理与控制系统术语

AFC	Auto Fare Collection	自动售检票系统
ATC	Automatic Train Control	列车自动控制
ATO	Automatic Train Operation	列车自动运行
ATP	Automatic Train Protection	列车自动防护
ATS	Automatic Train Supervision	列车自动监控
BAS	Building Automation System	建筑设备自动化系统
BCC	Backup Control Center	备用控制中心
FAS	Fire Alarm System	防灾报警系统

ISCS	Integrated Supervision and Control System	综合监控系统
MMI	Man Machine Interface	人机接口
OCC	Operated Control Center	控制中心
PIIS	Passenger Information and Indication System	旅客向导系统
PIS	Passenger Information System	乘客信息系统
SCADA	Scan Control Alarm Database	供电系统管理自动化
SSS	Subway Station Subsystem	车站子系统
TIMS	Train Integrated Management System	列车综合管理系统
TCMS	Train Control & Monitoring System	列车控制和监控系统
EOD	Equipment Operating Data	设备运行参数

二、车辆专业系统

APU	Audio Power Unit	放大器单元
AW0		空载
AW1		每位乘客都有座位
AW2		每平方米6人
AW3		每平方米9人
DVA	Digital and Audio Announcements	数字语音广播器
FDU	Frontal Display Unit	前部显示单元
IDU	Internal Display Unit	内部显示单元
LRU	Line Replaceable Unit	线路可替换单元
M(C)	Motor Car	动车
Mp(B)	Motor Car with Pantograph	带受电弓的动车
MPU	Main Processor Unit	主控单元
PB	Powered Bogie	动车转向架
RIOM	Remote Input Output Module	远程输入输出模块

TBD	To be Defined	待定义,待规定
TBEx	Trailer Bogie-External	拖车外转向架
TBIn	Train Bogie-Intermediate	拖车中间转向架
TBU	Tread Brake Unit	踏面制动单元
Tc(A)	Trailer Car	拖车
VPI	Visual Passenger Information	可视乘客信息
VVVF	Variable Voltage Variable Frequency	变压变频
WSP	Wheel Speed Sensor	轮速传感器

三、信号专业系统

ADM	Administrator Workstation	系统工作管理站
AR	Automatic Reversal	自动折返
ARS	Automatic Route Setting	列车自动进路排列
ATR	Automatic Train Regulation	列车自动调整
ATT	Automatic Train Tracking	列车自动跟踪
DTI	Departure Time Indicator	发车计时器
LCP	Local Control Panel	局部控制台
PTI	Positive Train Identification	列车自动识别
RM	Restricted Manual Mode	ATP限制允许速度的人工驾驶
SIC	Station Interface Case	车站接口箱
SICAS	Siemens Computer Aided Signaling	西门子计算机辅助信号

四、通信专业系统

CDD	Configuration and Data Distribution Server	配置及数字分配服务器
DDF	Digital Distribution Frame	数字配线架
DxTiP	Digital Exchange for TETRA	TETRA数字交换机
MDF	Multiplex Distribution Frame	综合配线架
NCC	Network Control Center	网络控制中心
ODF	Optical Distribution Frame	光配线架

OMS	OTN Management System	OTN 管理系统
PABX	Private Automatic Branch Exchange	专用自动小交换机
PCM	Pulse Code Modulation	脉冲编码调制
TBS	TETRA Base Station	TETRA 基站
TDM	Time Division Multiplexing	时分复用
TETRA	Terrestial Trunked Radio	欧洲数字集群标准
VDF	Audio Distribution Frame	音频配线架

五、自动售检票专业系统

CPS	Central Processing System	中央计算机系统
CSC	Contactless Smart Card	非接触智能卡
CST	Contactless Smart Token	非接触智能筹码
IDC	Intermodality Data Center	清结算数据中心
SPS	Station Processing System	车站计算机系统
PIN	Personal Identification Number	个人身份号码
TVM	Ticket Vending Machine	自动售票机
SEMI-TVM	Manually Operated Ticket Vending Machine	半自动售票机
PVU	Portable Verifying Unit	便携式验票机
GATE		闸机

六、火灾报警专业系统

FAC		消防专项合格证书
GCC	Graphic Control Computer	图形监视计算机

七、环境监控专业系统

EMCS	Electrical and Mechanical Control System	车站设备监控系统
ECS	Environment Control System	环境控制系统
DDC	Direct Digital Controller	数字直接控制器
PLC	Programmable Logic Controller	可编程逻辑控制器

八、综合监控专业系统

BISCS	Backup ISCS	备用综合监控系统
CISCS	Central ISCS	中央综合监控系统
FEP	Front End Processor	前端处理器
HMI	Human Machine Interface	人机界面
SISCS	Station ISCS	车站综合监控系统

九、技术术语

API	Application Programming Interface	应用程序接口
EMC	Electro Magnetic Compliance	电磁兼容性
FTP	File Transfer Protocol	文件传输协议
ISDN	Integrated Services Digital Network	综合业务数字网
LAN	Local Area Network	局域网
MCBF	Mean Cycles Between Failure	运行设备两次损坏之间的次数
MTBF	Mean Time Between Failures	平均无故障运行时间
MTTR	Mean Time To Repair	维修耗时平均值
OTN	Open Transport Network	开放传输网络
PSTN	Public Switched Telephone Network	公用电话交换网
TCP/IP	Transmission Control Protocol/Internet Protocol	传输控制/网络协议
UPS	Uninterrupted Power Supply	不间断电源供给
WAN	Wide Area Network	广域网

参考文献

[1] Sheilah Frey. Railway Electrification systems & engineering[M]. White World Publications, 2012.

[2] Pyrgidis Christos. Railway Transportation Systems [J]. Crc Press, 2016:161-170.

[3] 顾岷. 我国城市轨道交通发展现状与展望 [J]. 中国铁路, 2011: 53-56.

[4] 李建民. 城市轨道交通专业英语[M]. 2版. 北京:机械工业出版社,2016.

[5] 屈静,于燕红,张建荣. 民航机务职业英语口语[M]. 北京:机械工业出版社,2015.